BENCHLEY
—OR ELSE!

Also by Robert Benchley

ONE MINUTE PLEASE

BENCHLEY —OR ELSE!

by
ROBERT BENCHLEY

With Drawings by
Gluyas Williams

DENNIS DOBSON LIMITED · LONDON

First published in Great Britain in MCMXLVIII by DENNIS
DOBSON LTD, 12 Park Place, St James's, London
SW1. All rights reserved. Printed in Great Britain by
JARROLD & SONS LTD, Norwich.   120/R

Table of Contents

BENCHLEY

—OR ELSE!

Down with Pigeons

ST. FRANCIS OF ASSISI (unless I am getting him mixed up with St. Simeon Stylites, which might be very easy to do as both their names begin with "St.") was very fond of birds, and often had his picture taken with them sitting on his shoulders and pecking at his wrists. That was all right, if St. Francis liked it. We all have our likes and dislikes, and I have more of a feeling for dogs. However, I am not against birds as a class. I am just against pigeons.

I do not consider pigeons birds, in the first place. They are more in the nature of people; people who mooch. Probably my feeling about pigeons arises from the fact that all my life I have lived in rooms where pigeons came rumbling in and out of my window. I myself must have a certain morbid fascination for pigeons, because they follow me about so much—and with evident ill will. I am firmly convinced that they are trying to haunt me.

Although I live in the middle of a very large city (well, to show you how large it is—it is the largest in the world) I am awakened every morning by a low gargling sound which turns out to be the result of one, or two, or three pigeons walking in at my window and sneering at me. Granted that I am a fit subject for sneering as I lie there, possibly with one shoe on or an unattractive expression on my face, but there is something

1

more than just a passing criticism in these birds making remarks about me. They have some ugly scheme on foot against me, and I know it. Sooner or later it will come out, and then I can sue.

This thing has been going on ever since I was in college. In our college everybody was very proud of the

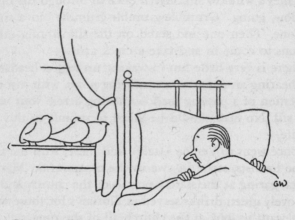

Pigeons walking in at my window and sneering at me

pigeons. Anyone walking across the Yard (Campus to you, please) was beset by large birds who insisted on climbing up his waistcoat and looking about in his wallet for nuts or raisins or whatever it is you feed pigeons (bichloride would be my suggestion, but let it pass).

God knows that I was decent enough to them in my undergraduate days. I let them walk up and down my back and I tried to be as nice as I could without actually letting them see that I was not so crazy about it. I even gave them chestnuts, chestnuts which I wanted myself.

2

I now regret my generosity, for good chestnuts are hard to get these days.

But somehow the word got around in pigeon circles that Benchley was antipigeon. They began pestering me. I would go to bed at night, tired from overstudy, and at six-thirty in the morning the Big Parade would begin. The line of march was as follows: Light on Benchley's window sill, march once in through the open window, going "Grumble-grumble-grumble" in a sinister tone. Then out and stand on the sill, urging other pigeons to come in and take a crack at it.

There is very little fun in waking up with a headache and hearing an ominous murmuring noise, with just the suggestion of a passing shadow moving across your window sill. No man should be asked to submit to this *all* his life.

I once went to Venice (Italy), and there, with the rest of the tourists, stood in awe in the center of St. Mark's Piazza, gazing at the stately portals of the church and at the lovely green drinks served at Florian's for those who don't want to look at the church all of the time.

It is an age-old custom for tourists to feed corn to the pigeons and then for the pigeons to crawl all over the tourists. This has been going on without interruption ever since Americans discovered Venice. So far as the records show, no pigeon has ever failed a tourist—and no tourist has ever failed a pigeon. It is a very pretty relationship.

In my case, however, it was different. In the first place, the St. Mark's pigeons, having received word from the American chapter of their lodge, began flying at me in such numbers and with such force as actually

I tried to be as nice as I could

to endanger my life. They came in great droves, all flying low and hard, just barely skimming my hat and whirring in an ugly fashion with some idea of intimidating me. But by that time I was not to be intimidated, and, although I ducked very low and lost my hat several times, I did not give in. I even bought some corn from one of the vendors and held it out in my hand, albeit with bad grace. But, for the first time in centuries, no pigeon fell for the corn gag. I stood alone in the middle of St. Mark's square, holding out my hand dripping with kernels of golden corn, and was openly and deliberately snubbed. One or two of the creatures walked up to within about ten feet of me and gave me a nasty look, but not one gave my corn a tumble. So I decided the hell with them and ate the corn myself.

Now this sort of thing must be the result of a very definite boycott, or, in its more aggressive stage, an anti-Benchley campaign. Left to myself, I would have only the very friendliest feelings for pigeons (it is too late now, but I might once have been won over). But having been put on my mettle, there is nothing that I can do now but fight back. Whatever I may be, I am not yellow.

Here is my plan. I know that I am alone in this fight, for most people like pigeons, or, at any rate, are not antagonized by them. But single-handed I will take up the cudgels, and I hope that, when they grow up, my boys will carry on the battle on every cornice and every campus in the land.

Whenever I meet a pigeon, whether it be on my own window sill or walking across a public park, I will stop still and place my hands on my hips and wait. If the pigeon wants to make the first move and attack me, I will definitely strike back, even to the extent of hitting it with my open palm and knocking it senseless (not a very difficult feat, I should think, as they seem to have very little sense).

I have worked up a noise which . . . is just as unpleasant sounding as theirs

If they prefer to fight it out by innuendo and sneering, I will fight it out by innuendo and sneering. I have worked up a noise which I can make in my throat which is just as unpleasant sounding as theirs. I will even take advantage of my God-given power of speech and will say: "Well, what do you want to make of it, you waddling, cooing so-and-sos?" I will glare at them just as they glare at me, and if they come within reach of my foot, so help me, St. Francis, I will kick at them. *And* the next pigeon that strolls in across my window ledge when I am just awakening, I will catch with an especially prepared trap and will drag into my room, there to punch the living daylights out of him.

I know that this sounds very cruel and very much as if I were an animal hater. As a matter of fact, I am such a friend of animals in general that I am practically penniless. I have been known to take in dogs who were obviously impostors and put them through college. I am a sucker for kittens, even though I know that one day they will grow into cats who will betray and traduce me. I have even been known to pat a tiger cub, which accounts for my writing this article with my left hand.

But as far as pigeons go, I am through. It is a war to the death, and I have a horrible feeling that the pigeons are going to win.

"Awake,
Awake!"

THE art of awakening people out of a sound sleep is one which needs a little refining. There is too much cruelty abroad. Being awakened at all is bad enough without having it done by a gorilla.

I don't suppose we should blame the Pullman porter because he gives those four vicious tugs at the bottom of your blanket. When it happens, I could leap from my berth and strangle him with my bare hands, but, as I lie there determining to go back to sleep just to spite him, I realize that of all people, Pullman porters have a right to be peremptory in their signals that it is time to get up. With a whole carful of sleepers to whip into shape, they must have a pretty tough time of it.

Sometime I would like to read an article by a Pullman porter detailing the responses—and percentage of direct successes—he gets on his morning rounds. There is a man who sees human nature at its worst.

But, granting the porter's right to make a beast of himself at awakening his charges, who else is justified in being uncharitable about the act? Certainly not friends or relatives of the sleeper. And yet among these we find the worst offenders.

There are some people who undergo a complete change of nature when it comes time to get someone else

8

out of bed. Ordinarily they may be sweet-natured, considerate Christians, loath to offend and slow to command. But when the time comes to awaken somebody, a fiendish gleam comes into their eyes and their hands twitch in anticipation.

"Let me get him up," they sometimes beg. "I'll do it." Two fangs appear over their under lips and a hump on their backs, and they tiptoe to the bedroom where the unsuspecting victim is lying, like vampires on some grisly errand.

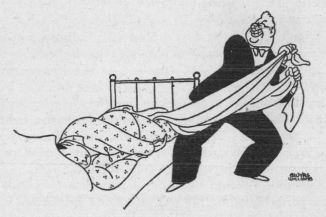

"Come on, come on!" they shout with glee

"Come on, come on!" they shout with glee. "Time to get up!" With this, and before the sleeper has a chance to scowl and gag himself into consciousness, they yank the covers back or shake him violently by the shoulder. The late Jack Pickford had a little whimsey of firing a revolver off in the room of the sleeper. This I do not consider one-tenth as despicable as the personal attacks

9

of those who pretend that they are doing only their duty. A revolver fired to awaken a man is definitely a violation of all codes, a thing so horrendous as almost to be funny. There is no pretense of being anything but a cad of the first water, and I am not so sure that, if awakening has got to be performed, a good revolver shot by the ear is not the kindest method to adopt. At any rate, the sleeper doesn't have those first awful seconds

He will have the consolation of knowing that he has behaved like a gentleman

when he thinks that maybe, if he were to pretend to be dead, he would eventually be let alone. He knows that he is dead.

But the hypocrites who, already being awake, cannot bear to see anyone else sleeping, and yet have not the nerve to shoot a gun off, but must pretend that they are doing it for your own good—these are the abominations. As they leer down at you, after their vicious "Come on!"

10

so smug in their superiority and so sure that they are "doing the right thing," they represent the worst element in our civilization—the Brother's Keeper.

If anyone feels that he has to awaken me, I would suggest that he purchase a set of those mellifluous dinner chimes or a small harp, and walk slowly up and down beside my bed, playing something that he knows how to play. It may take a few minutes to bring me to, or it may take a couple of hours, but he will at least have the consolation of knowing that he has behaved like a gentleman and not an unconscionable boor.

And, besides, why does anyone feel that he has to awaken me at all? Did I ever ask to be awakened?

The Helping Hand

I HAVE always tried to be as public-spirited as I could and yet save out a little time to myself for running and jumping. That is, when the Fuel Administration wanted us all to save coal, I saved coal with a will; when it was Anti-Litter Week, I anti-littered; when the nation was supposed to be devoting itself to eating apples, I drank applejack until the cows came home—and very funny-looking cows they were, too.

So when the head of the Unemployment Commission came out over the radio and asked every good citizen to set about "sprucing up" his home and give employment to as many men as possible, I saw my duty and set about doing it.

My house could stand a little "sprucing up," for we have been hoping to sell it for eight or ten years (centrally located in Westchester County, three minutes from the station, colonial type, four master's bedrooms and three masters, servants' quarters at the foot of the plantation equipped with banjos and corn pone, two chimneys, of which one is imitation; just try naming a price and see what happens), and when you expect to sell a house any minute you more or less put off "sprucing up." So I figured that I could help out the situation considerably merely by fixing up the house so that the owls didn't fly in through the roof at night.

Aside from having the roof patted down, I decided

that a couple of eaves troughs could stand a little humoring; that one of the master's bathtubs might very well be given a new porcelain filling; that the furnace could easily be looked into by an expert, possibly using a ferret to get out that clinker which got stuck in the grate four years ago; and that we needed a new lock on the front door (or perhaps it was a new key; at any rate, the front door couldn't be locked).

This shaped up like quite a boon to the unemployed of the town. All that remained was for me myself to find enough work to do to pay for it.

We had quite a little trouble in finding a carpenter and a plumber who could promise to come before the following week (no matter how serious the unemployment situation, no individual carpenter or plumber can ever come before the following week, doubtless out of habit), and the locksmith and the furnaceman just didn't seem interested. But we finally got a little group of experts who agreed to drop in the next day and see what could be done.

In the meantime, we had discovered that the electric range needed tampering with and that a fresh coat of paint wouldn't hurt the back porch. So we engaged an electrician and a painter to come in the next day also.

The next day was one of those crisp late fall days when everyone feels so good that he wants to stay right in bed under the blankets all the morning. I was surprised, therefore, in my bathrobe by Mr. Margotson, the carpenter, and Mr. Rallif, the electrician, who arrived together at eight-thirty. This started the thing off on an informal basis right at the beginning, and as Mr. Shrank, the locksmith, came a few minutes later, it seemed only hospitable to ask them if they wouldn't like a second cup of coffee before starting to work. At this point the furnaceman, Mr. Thurple, arrived in the painter's automobile (I didn't quite catch the painter's name, but I thing it was Schnee; at any rate, I called him Schnee and he seemed quite pleased), and so our little coffee party was now six, including the host, which just filled the breakfast table nicely.

"Do you take cream in your coffee, Mr. Margotson?" I asked. Mr. Margotson and Mr. Rallif having been the first to arrive, it seemed to me that they should be served first.

"It's strange that you should have asked me that," replied Mr. Margotson, "for I was saying to Mrs. Margotson at breakfast only this morning, 'I see in the paper where a man says that cream *and* sugar together in coffee set up a poison which sooner or later results in a toxæmia!'"

"Don't you think," put in Mr. Thurple, helping himself to cream and sugar, "that we are, as a nation, becoming a little too self-conscious about what we eat and drink? As a nation, I mean."

Mr. Schnee, or whatever his name was, laughed a low, tinkling laugh. This, although Mr. Schnee said nothing, somehow broke the ice and we all laughed. I had never seen five more congenial and delightful men together at one table (six, if you want to count me; I couldn't very well have said it of myself). As soon as we all had our coffee cups well poised, the conversation became general and drifted from dietetics to religion and then quickly back to dietetics again. When Mr. Ramm, the plumber (true to the jokes in the funny papers, the last to arrive), came bursting in he found us deep in a discussion of whether or not ransom should be paid in kidnaping cases.

"The late Mr. Ramm!" taunted Mr. Thurple, the furnaceman, who had already established himself as the clown of the crowd by having seven cups of coffee. At which sally Mr. Schnee again laughed his low, tinkling laugh and set us all off again. As soon as Mr. Ramm had recovered from his embarrassment at being the butt of Mr. Thurple's joke, I set the round of the day's activities in motion.

"How many here play badminton?" I asked, springing to my feet.

"I," "I," and "I," came with a will from three hearty throats, and Messrs. Margotson, Rallif, and Thurple had their coats off and their sleeves rolled up as an earnest of their intentions.

"Take me, I like backgammon," said Mr. Ramm.

"You're my man then," said Mr. Shrank. "I am the backgammon king of Locksmiths' Row." It looked for a minute as if we were in for a rather nasty argument, but Mr. Schnee's low, musical laugh came again to the rescue, and the party was on. The room which had been full of men only a minute before was now emptied in a trice, some rushing pell-mell to the badminton court and some to the backgammon room.

Luncheon was a gay affair, with favors for those who had won at their various games and speeches of acceptance which convulsed even the low-laughing Mr. Schnee.

"I am sorry, gentlemen," I said, in part, when it came my turn, "that I have got you all here to do certain jobs to which you are severally suited by training and study, for I find that I have not the money to pay you with, even if you were to carry out your commissions. But what there is of good cheer and good fellowship in this house is yours, and we are all going to make the most of it while it lasts."

That was a month and a half ago and they are all still living with me. We are the best of friends and still the small boys at heart that we always were. The house is in much worse condition than it was before; but, as it turned out that they all had more money than I, I am not worrying. They have each promised to buy a story from me as soon as I can get around to writing it.

Stop Those Hiccoughs!

ANYONE will be glad to admit that he knows nothing about beagling, or the Chinese stock market, or ballistics, but there is not a man or woman alive who does not claim to know how to cure hiccoughs. The funny thing is that the hiccoughs are never cured until they get darned good and ready.

The most modest and unassuming man in the world becomes an arrogant know-it-all in the presence of hiccoughs—in somebody else.

"Don't be silly," he says, patronizingly. "Just put your head under your arm, hold a glass of water against the back of your neck, and count to five hundred by fives without taking a breath. It never fails."

* * * * *

Then, when it *has* failed, he blames you. "It's absolutely sure-fire if you only follow my directions," he says. He also implies darkly that what is ailing you is not just merely hiccoughs. "My method can't be expected to cure drunkenness, you know," he says.

To date, I have been advised to perform the following feats to cure hiccoughs:

Bend the body backward until the head touches the floor, and whistle in reverse.

Place the head in a pail of water and inhale twelve times deeply.

17

Drink a glass of milk from the right hand with the right arm twisted around the neck until the milk enters the mouth from the left side.

Hop, with the feet together, up and down a flight of steps ten times, screaming loudly at each hop.

Roll down a long, inclined lawn, snatching a mouthful of grass up each time the face is downward.

I have tried them all, with resultant torn ligaments, incipient drowning, lockjaw and arsenic poisoning, but, each time, at the finish of the act, and a few seconds of waiting while my mentor says, triumphantly: "See! What did I tell you?" that one, big hiccough always breaks the tension, indicating that the whole performance has been a ghastly flop.

* * * * *

The most unassuming man becomes an arrogant know-it-all in the presence of hiccoughs

My latest fiasco came as the result of reading the prescription of a Boston doctor, and almost resulted in my being put away as an irresponsible person. "All that the sufferer has to do," wrote the doctor, "is to blow up an ordinary paper bag, as if to explode it and then hold it over the mouth and nose tightly, breathing in and out of the bag instead of in and out of the open air."

This, according to the doctor, creates an excess of carbon monoxide gas in the bag, which is breathed over and over again, acting on a nervous center of the brain and curing the hiccoughs.

I blew the bag up and held
it tightly over my face

Being alone in the room at the time, I blew the bag up and held it tightly over my face, including not only my mouth and nose, but my eyes as well, like a gas mask. I subjected myself to this treatment for possibly three minutes, walking around the room at the same time to keep from getting bored.

*   *   *   *   *

When I removed the bag I found myself the object of the silent but terrified scrutiny of my wife, who had entered the room without my knowing it, and who had already motioned for corroborating witnesses from the next room, two of whom were standing in the doorway, transfixed.

My explanation that I was curing hiccoughs did not go very big, as what I had obviously been doing was walking around the room alone with a paper bag over my head. This is *not* a good sign.

Incidentally, I still have my hiccoughs.

J'Accuse

LET'S have an end of all this shilly-shallying. *I* killed Rasputin. The thing has dragged on long enough, with even Mike Romanoff claiming that he did it, and my uncle claiming that it was done by the boys of his curling-club. Well, as a matter of fact, I am the one who did it, and here is how it happened.

We were sitting around in the cellar of the Winter Palace, Rasputin, Mike Romanoff, a Grand Duke whose name I have forgoten, and I. We had a couple of dancing bears in for the occasion, and things were beginning to get a little rowdy.

According to a pre-arranged plan between Mike Romanoff and myself, a tray of *hors d'oeuvres* was brought in for us to dip in our vodka. Each canape consisted of a little mound of elk-poison, covered with grated egg, and to make things safer, the egg had been poisoned, too. Four elk had been killed in the out-of-town try out, so Mike and I were in high good humor.

Naturally, the tray was passed first to Rasputin, for, if anyone else was served first, he was one mad monk, I can tell you. He took four canapes in one hand and two in the other, and put them all in his mouth at once. I took one and palmed it, and Mike said: "No, thanks. They're so much poison to me," which I thought was a pretty funny crack, coming from Mike. By this time, all eyes were on Rasputin.

He wiped the crumbs from his beard, took a swig of vodka, and said: "'Those are mighty nice cookies. Where did you get them?" Then he got up and went to the window and looked out. "It looks like snow," he said. "By George, it *is* snow!" And he danced up and down in delight to see the little flakes swirling down through the air. Those Russians are just like kids when it starts to snow.

I looked at Mike and he shrugged his shoulders. "Mike," I said, "how about whamming old Rasputin over the head with that iron bell-clapper, just to see if he likes butter?"

Rasputin turned to see what was up, just as Mike crashed down on him with the heavy clapper we had taken from the church of St. Sophia earlier that day. The hair on the Mad Monk's head went down so far that it got into the hair of his beard, but he opened up a little space in it with his fingers, and said:

"Come on, cut out this kidding! I've got work to do this afternoon, even if you boys haven't."

"You try it, Bob," said Mike, trying to dislodge the clapper. So I took out my gun, and holding Rasputin at arm's length, said: "One to get ready—two to start— and three to go—o!" I fired four times into him, and hit him over the head with the gun-butt for the pay-off. I have never seen a guy so sore in my life.

"Hey, what is this?" he said. "Let somebody else be It for a while. I'm all out of breath." So I made believe that we were friends again, and put my arm around his shoulder.

"O. K., Rasputin," I said, "let bygones be bygones, and don't be a baby all your life. What about a little stroll down to the lake to throw fire-crackers at the fish?"

He was pleased as punch at the idea, and we walked arm in arm, down to the lake, which was frozen over, except around the edges. Rasputin tried to hypnotize me on the way, but I slapped him down. "None of your mad monk-ey business," I said, and, while he was laughing at my play on words, I rolled him under the edge of the ice so far that I had to put skates on to get out to where he was.

I skated around him for a while, cutting figure eights, until Mike joined me, and then we two went fishing through the ice for him, Every time we caught him, we threw him back, until finally, tiring of our sport, we replaced the block of ice over the hole, stamped it down and left him.

Now that is the true story of how Rasputin was killed, and I don't think there's a jury in the country that would convict me. So let's have no more talk about it, please.

Inherent Vice: Express Paid

SOME evening, when you haven't anything to read, why not light a cozy fire, draw up your chair, and browse around among your old express receipts and bills of lading? You will learn a lot. Here you have been going on for years, sending parcels and crates like mad, and I'll bet that not one of you really knows the contractual obligations you have been entering into with the companies who serve you. For all you know, you have been agreeing to marry the company manager at the end of sixty days.

As I write this, I am sitting in the gloaming of a late autumn afternoon with an express company's receipt on the table before me. As I read over the fine print on the back of it, my eyes cross gradually with the strain and I put on the light. (What a wonderful invention—electricity! I am sure that we should all be very proud and happy to be living in this age.)

As my eyes adjust themselves, I find that when I sent that old bureau to Ruth's folks, I agreed to let the express company get away with the following exceptions to their liability. (If you are going to read this article, I would advise studying the following. It will probably amuse you more than what I have to sav afterward.)

The company shall in no event be liable for any loss, damage, or delay to said property or to any part thereof occasioned by act of God, by perils or accidents of the sea or

24

other waters, [That "others waters" makes a pretty broad exemption, when you come to think of it. It means that they can upset tumblers on your stuff, or let roguish employees play squirt guns all over it, and yet not be responsible.] or of navigation or transportation of whatsoever nature or kind; by fire or explosion . . . by theft or pilferage [What about garroting?] by any person whatsoever; by arrest or restraint of governments, princes, rulers, or peoples or those purporting to exercise governmental or other authority; by legal process or stoppage in transit; by fumigation or other acts or requirements of quarantine or sanitary authorities; [Tell me when you are getting tired.] by epidemics, pestilence, riots, or rebellions; by war or any of the dangers incident to a state of war, or by acts of any person or group of persons purporting to wage war or to act as a belligerent; [Come, come, Mr. Express Company—aren't you being just a little bit picayune?] by strikes or stoppage of labor or labor troubles, whether of carrier's employees or others; by unseaworthiness of any vessel, lighter, or other craft whatsoever, [Not even just a teeny-weeny bit of a rowboat?] although existing at the time of shipment on board thereof; . . . by water, [You said that once before.] heating, or the effects of climate, frost, decay, smell, taint, rust, sweat, dampness, mildew, spotting, rain or spray, [Ninety-five-a-hundred-all around my goal are it.] INHERENT VICE, [Remember that one; we're coming back to that later.] drainage, leakage, vermin, improper or insufficient packing, inaccuracies or obliterations, errors, [Why don't they just say "errors" and let it go at that?] nor for the breakage of any fragile articles or damage to any materials consisting of or contained in glass; nor shall this company [Beginning all over again, in case you should have forgotten who it is that isn't responsible.] be held liable or responsible for any damage to or resulting from dangerous corrosives, explosives, or inflammable goods, even if the true nature has been declared to the company; nor for neglect, damage, accident to or escape or mortality of any animals or birds [Ah-ha! They forgot fish!] received by the company hereunder, from any cause whatsoever.

That's all! Aside from that, the express company is responsible for your package.

Aside from that, your little crate or barrel is as safe as it would be in your own home. It would almost be better to get a sled and drag your package yourself to wherever you want it taken.

At least, you could personally fight off vermin and princes (or those purporting to be vermin and princes).

But the thing that worries me most about this contract between me and the express company is that clause about "inherent vice."

The company is not responsible for any damage to that bureau of mine if it is caused by inherent vice. This makes you stop and think.

Wholly aside from the Calvinistic dourness of the phrase "inherent vice" (I thought that the theory of Original Sin and Inherent Vice went out with the hanging of witches), the question now arises—*whose* inherent vice? The company's officials? The bureau's? Aunt Alice's? We are up against quite a nice problem in ethics here.

I can't imagine what you could send by express that would be full enough of inherent vice to damage it en route. Certainly nothing that you could pack in a bureau.

You might send some very naughty rabbits or squirrels by express, but it seems a little narrow-minded to put all the responsibility for their actions on the little creatures themselves. No one has ever told them that they are vicious, or that they were conceived in sin. They don't *know* that they are being bad.

I have known one or two very smart dogs who were pretty self-conscious about being wicked and couldn't look you in the eye afterward, but aside from cases like that it seems a bit arbitrary for a big public-service corporation like an express company to frown on the peccadillos of five or six squirrels.

Would the private lives of the company officials themselves bear looking into so well that they must prate of inherent vice? Live and let live, say I.

Which brings us to the other theory—that inherent vice in the company's officials or employees cannot be held responsible for any damage to my bureau.

Do you mean to tell me that if one of the company's employees is a man who, ever since he was a boy, has been willfully and maliciously destructive, and that if he takes my bureau out of its crate and chops the whole thing up into kindling—do you mean to tell me that I am without recourse to the law?

If the president of the express company or any one of his employees goes monkeying around with my bureau and then pleads "not guilty" because of his inherent vice, I will start a *putsch* that will bring our government crashing down around our ears.

I refuse to discuss the remaining possibility—that the inherent vice referred to means inherent vice in Aunt Alice, or consignee.

This brings us to the conclusion that what is meant

is that the package or bale or crate (or articles purporting to be packages, or bales, or crates) might have inherent vice enough to spoil it, and that, in this event, the company washes its hands of the whole affair.

The only alternative to this almost incredibly silly reservation is that there has been a misprint, and that what the company is so afraid of is "inherent *mice*." In this case, I have taken up all your time for nothing. But I do think that you ought to know what you are agreeing to when you send an express package. Or perhaps you don't care.

Botany Exam

HOW many of my little readers, on walking (with an occasional hop, skip, and jump, no doubt) through Central Park have ever been confronted suddenly by what I call "Examination Grove"? . . . I am afraid that I haven't made myself clear.

South of the Reservoir, on the west side of the Park, just before you begin to wonder if it wouldn't be better if you took a cab for the rest of the way, is a little path which wanders with no valid excuse between a line of trees and shrubs in a direction south-by-southeast from that in which you want to be going.

These trees and shrubs have all been labeled in the customary flip manner by the horticulturists, to whom a tree is not so much a tree as a third-declension Latin noun with its modifying adjective, but they have not stopped at this impertinence, Each tree and shrub is hung with a little tag bearing a question, presumably addressed to the hitherto carefree stroller. Thus, the tender sapling on your right not only has to bear its foliage and perhaps a great hulking bird in its branches, but also a sign reading: "How can the leaves of the pink oak be recognized?" Yonder rock which beckons so temptingly to the weary wanderer (known as "Beckoning Rock" among the natives) is made impossible for resting purposes by a tag which demands peremptorily to know: "What kind of moss is found on this kind of rock?" The City of New York in its paternalism, not content with Nature's supply of books in the running brooks and sermons in stones, has taken on itself the task of making examination papers of its trees and shrubs. Could the preceptorial spirit go further? (Take three minutes to answer this question.)

The first time I ran upon these posers I was naturally thrown into something of a panic. Being conscientious

to a fault in matters of civic duty, I had a feeling that I ought to answer them all before I could pass through the reservation. For years I had been a beneficiary of the City of New York, accepting its police-protection (no tittering, please), its street-lighting and its playgrounds. The least that I could do now was to answer a few simple questions in return.

But the very first one which had caught my attention, attached to a small shrub and reading: "Where is another shrub similar to this, and what is its name?" gave me a guilty feeling of being under suspicion of having hidden the other shrub myself, when, as a matter of fact, this was the first I had known of the whole affair. I retraced my steps, looking for something which might resemble the shrub in question, but there was nothing. I had failed miserably on my very first question, so there was nothing for me to do but take my pencil and write "Sorry" on the tag and go back to the main pathway. All the way home in the cab (I really didn't feel like walking any more after that) I sobbed as if my little heart would break.

Since then I have grown hardened and often walk through "Examination Grove," trying not to look at the questions. But the place is spoiled for me. I cannot pass that rock without thinking: "You don't know what kind of moss is found on that kind of rock. You don't know *anything* and you never will. Exeter, Harvard, the Sorbonne, Heidelberg—what good did they do you? You don't even know how to recognize the leaves of the pink oak." Often I rush from there to the lake and row furiously about in a boat, trying to relieve my inferiority by an excess of physical exertion, but in my heart I know that Mayor Walker would be just as disappointed in me as he could be, were he to find out how I had failed him.

My nightmare now is that the City of New York, crazed with its success in botany quizzing, will take to popping questions at me about other items of its equipment. Suppose one day I were to come across a hydrant bearing a tag reading: "What pressure would be necessary to project this stream fifty feet through this opening (6 in. diameter)?" or an iron lamp-post asking: "What is the coefficient of linear expansion of this metal?" Imagine my embarrassment! Imagine your own, for you, too, are involved in the menace of this teacher-complex on the part of the City Fathers.

The only way in which we, as citizens, can get back at our tormentors is to ask them questions in return. We may not be erudite in our questions, but we can be embarrassing. We can put a sign over that hole in Forty-fourth Street asking: "How much macadam would it take to fill up this hole, and why the hell isn't it done?" On every street corner we could stick up little signs reading: "What belongs here for the reception of waste-paper?" and on the backs of some policeman we could pin signs: "What has this policeman been drinking, where did he get it, and did it conform with the Municipal Bureau of Standards' test for 'legal' liquor?" And, of course, if we were mean enough, we could string a banner across Seventh Avenue at the Park Central Hotel asking, in red letters, "Let's see—who was it who killed Arnold Rothstein?"

Oh, there are plenty of questions that we could ask if once we started. We may not know what kind of moss grows on what kind of rock, but we are no fools.

End of the Chanticleer!

FOR the benefit of those who find themselves unable to sleep through the early-morning clarion call of the rooster (sometimes called "The Herald of the Dawn," among other names), I will recount how I, single-handed, put an end to this chanticleer business for at least one morning.

In telling my story I may have to make myself seem to be cutting a rather strange figure, but I am willing to be misunderstood if I can spread the word that the Lord of the Barnyard need no longer also be the Lord of the Bedroom, and that a man, by striking out with some spirit, can meet a rooster in single combat, and win.

* * * * *

Returning home late from a Grange meeting, I was shown to the guest-room which, as it turned out, was abutting the poultry reservation. I had barely found my pillow (it was a small one and easily lost) and closed my eyes (also small and easily lost) when Sir Rooster began to put on his act. "Cock-a-doodle-do" is the way it is printed, but that is a euphemism.

At first I thought that the bird was in bed with me, but, after a careful pawing with my hands and feet, I decided that he was outside. It then became a matter for direct action on my part. With a determination which I seldom display in crises, I got out of bed and, putting on the tops of my pajamas, went out into the hen-yard.

I took my stand by the wire enclosure and waited. Several of the hens paid me the courtesy of a glance, but the rooster was gathering himself for another onslaught at the silences and did not see me. I was calmness itself.

*   *   *   *   *

Then it came—a rousing, throaty crow, which he doubtless thought was causing me to writhe on my couch inside the guest-house. I did not leave him long in his fool's paradise. I answered him with a louder and throatier crow which practically tore my tonsils from their moorings, but which also sent my antagonist toppling to one side in surprise and chagrin. The battle was on!

Every time he crowed I would crow back, going him one better. Once I even carried the fight into his own territory and crowed first. This sent him into a fever of inferiority, believe it or not. The Cock of the Walk befuddled, confused, and a tantrum of futility!

The hens took it rather hard. Not only were they being terrified personally (I saw to that, in my odd moments), but their hero was being mocked, ridiculed, and outplayed at his own game. They ran to and fro in despair, but I was not to be put off by any considerations of chivalry. I even did a few hen cackles to put *them* in *their* places. It was a complete rout in favor of the forces of law and order.

*   *   *   *   *

It was not long before I waited in vain for a "cock-a-doodle-do" to set me off into my own. The rooster was licked and he knew it. A few hens were still loyal to him and tried to curry favor by running back to him and saying, "The man's drunk! Pay no attention to him." But I wasn't drunk, unless it was with power, and the Old Devil knew it.

So, still in the tops of my pajamas, I made my triumphal entry back into the guest-house and took a well-deserved nap, with no sound from the hen-yard except a few scattered cluckings from discontented poultry who were talking it over. The Big Shot was silent, probably committing suicide.

I found out at luncheon, however, that I had awakened everyone else in the household, which somehow was never completely under the spell of the illusion that I was a rooster. Well, in every great cause some few innocent heads must fall.

Ladies Wild

IN THE exclusive set (no diphtheria cases allowed) in which I travel, I am known as a heel in the matter of parlor games. I will drink with them, wrassle with them and, now and again, leer at the ladies, but when they bring out the bundles of pencils and the pads of paper and start putting down all the things they can think of beginning with "W," or enumerating each other's bad qualities on a scale of 100 (no hard-feeling results, mind you—just life-long enmity), I tip-toe noisily out of the room and say: "The hell with you."

For this reason, I am not usually included in any little games that may be planned in advance. If they foresee an evening of "Consequences" coming over them, they whisper "Get Benchley out of the house. Get him a horse to ride, or some beads to string—anything to get him out of the way." For, I forgot to tell you, not only am I a non-participant in parlor games, but I am a militant non-participant. I heckle from the sidelines. I throw stones and spit at the players. Hence the nick-name: "Sweet Old Bob," or sometimes just the initials.

One night last summer, I detected, from the general stir among the ladies and more effete gents, that I was being eased out of the house. This meant that the gaming was about to begin. But instead of the usual clatter of pencils among the *croupiers*, I saw someone sneaking in with a tray of poker chips. They almost had me out the door when I discovered what was up.

"Well, so long, Bob," they said. "Good bowling to you."

"What's this?" I came back into the room. "Are those poker chips?"

"Sure, they're poker chips. It's all right to play poker, isn't it? The reform administration's gone out."

I assumed a hurt air. In fact, I didn't have to assume it. I was hurt.

"I don't suppose I'm good enough to play poker with you," I said. "All I'm good enough for is to furnish the liquor and the dancing girls."

"Why, we thought you didn't like games. You always act like such a goddamned heel whenever a game is suggested."

"My dear people," I said, trying to be calm, "there are games and games. 'Twenty Questions' is one game, if you will, but poker—why, poker is a man's game. It's my dish. I'm an old newspaperman, you know. Poker is the breath of life to a newspaperman." (As a matter of fact, I never played poker once when I was on a newspaper, and was never allowed to do more than kibitz at the Thanatopsis games of Broun, Adams, Kaufman, and that bunch, but poker is still my favorite game in a small way, or at least it *was*.)

Then there was a great scrambling to get me a chair, and sell me chips. "Old Bob's going to play!" was the cry. "Old Bob likes poker!" People came in from the next room to see what the commotion was, and one woman said that, if I was going to play, she had a headache. (I had ruined a game of "Who Am I?" for

37

"This is the real poker costume," I said

her once by blowing out a fuse from the coat-closet.)

As for me, I acted the part to the hilt. I took off my coat, unbuttoned my vest so that just the watch-chain connected it, lighted my pipe, and kept my hat on the back of my head.

"This is the real poker costume," I said. "The way we used to play it down on the old Trib. There ought to be a City News ticker over in the corner to make it seem like home."

"I'm afraid he's going to be too good for us," said one of the more timid ladies. "We play for very small stakes, you know."

"The money doesn't matter," I laughed. "It's the game. And anyway," I added modestly, "I haven't played for a long time. You'll probably take me good." (I wish now that I had made book on that prediction.)

It was to be Dealer's Choice, which should have given me a tip-off right there, with three women at the table, one the dealer.

"This," she announced, looking up into space as if for inspiration, "is going to be 'Hay Fever.' "

"I beg pardon," I said leaning forward.

" 'Hay Fever,' " explained one of the men. "The girls like it. One card up, two down, the last two up. One-eyed Jacks, sevens, and nines wild. High-low."

"I thought this was going to be poker," I said.

"From then on you play it just like regular poker," said the dealer.

From then on! My God! Just like regular poker!

Having established myself as an old poker-fan, I didn't want to break down and cry at the very start so I played the hand through. I say I "played" it. I sat looking at my cards, peeking now and then just to throw a bluff that I knew what I was doing. One-eyed Jacks, sevens, and nines wild, I kept saying that to myself, and puffing very hard at my pipe. After a minute of owlish deliberation, I folded.

The next hand was to be "Whistle Up Your Windpipe," another one which the girls had introduced into the group and which the men, weak-kneed sissies that they were, had allowed to become regulation. This was seven-card stud, first and last cards up, deuces, treys, and red-haired Queens wild, high-low-and-medium. I figured out that I had a very nice straight, bet it as I would have bet straight in the old days, and was beaten to eleven dollars and sixty cents by a royal straight flush. Amid general laughter, I was told that an ordinary straight in these games is worth no more than a pair of sixes in regular poker. A royal straight flush usually wins. Well, it usually won in the old days, too.

By the time the deal came to me, my pipe had gone out and I had taken my hat off. Between clenched teeth I announced: "And this, my frands, is going to be something *you* may not have heard of. This is going to be *old-fashioned draw-poker*, with *nothing* wild." The women had to have it explained to them, and remarked that they didn't see much fun in that. However, the hand was played. Nobody had anything (in comparison to what they had been having in the boom days), and nobody bet. The hand was over in a minute and a half, amid terrific silence.

That was the chief horror of this epidemic of "Whistle Up Your Windpipe," "Beezy-Weezy," and "Mice Afloat." It made old-fashioned stud seem tame, even to me. Every time it came to me, I elected the old game, just out of spite, but nobody's heart was in it. I became the spoil-sport of the party again, and once or twice I caught them trying to slip the deal past me, as if by mistake. Even a round of jack-pots netted nothing in the way of excitement, and even when I won one on a full-house, there was no savor to the victory, as I had to explain to the women what a full-house was. They thought that I was making up my own rules. Nothing as small as a full-house had ever been seen in that game.

The Big Newspaper Man was taken for exactly sixty-one dollars and eight cents when the game broke up at four A. M. Two of the women were the big winners. They had finally got it down to a game where everything was wild but the black nines, and everyone was trying for "low."

From now on I not only walk out on "Twenty Questions" and "Who Am I?" but, when there are ladies present (God *bless* them!), I walk out on poker. And a fine state of affairs it is when an old newspaper man has to walk out on poker!

Sporting Life in America

Following the Porter

HAVING someone carry your bag for you is a form of sport which has only comparatively recently found favor in America. It has come with the effemination of our race and the vogue of cuffs attached to the shirt.

When I was a boy (and I remember President Franklin Pierce saying, "What a boy!" too) to let a porter carry your bag was practically the same as saying: "My next imitation will be of Miss Jenny Lind, the Swedish Nightingale." No man who could whistle or chin himself would think of it. In the days before these new-fangled steam cars started raising Old Ned with our apple orchards with their showers of sparks, I have seen men knock a porter down for even reaching for their valises. The only people who would consider such a thing were veterans of the Mexican War who had lost both arms above the elbow or traveling salesmen for pipe-organ concerns. The traveling salesmen could let a porter take one end of the pipe organ without incurring the sneers of their fellow travelers.

But nowadays it is a pretty unattractive porter who can't wheedle a great hulking man out of his brief case, even if he is just crossing a platform to take another train. And I am secretly glad of this change in the standards of virility; for, frankly, my arms used to get awfully tired in the old days. This was due, in part, to the fact that any suitcase I ever buy always weighs a minimum of sixty pounds without anything in it. It is something about belonging to *me* that makes a suitcase put on weight. I lift other people's suitcases and they are like thistledown. But mine, with perhaps two collars and a tube of shaving cream in it, immediately swells up and behaves like the cornerstone of a twenty-story building. I know that this is not just my imagination, because several people have tried to steal my suitcase and have complained to me about its being so heavy.

But even now I still have a slightly guilty feeling as I walk up the runway with a porter going on ahead with my bags. I try to look as if I were not with him, or as if he had snatched up my luggage by mistake and I were trying to catch him to take it myself. If it is very obvious that he is with me, I carry my right arm as if I had just hurt it badly. You can't blame a cripple for not carrying his own bag.

It is not only the impression that I must be making on other people that worries me. I feel a little guilty about the porter. If the bag is very heavy (as it always is, and not from what you think, either) I start out with a slightly incoherent apology to him, like: "You'll find that pretty heavy, I'm afraid," or "Don't do this if you don't really feel like it." Sometimes I tell him what I have in the bag, so that he will understand. "Books," I say, timidly. (He never believes this.) I have even been so specific, if the thing was very heavy, as to tell him that I was carrying home a law digest and a copy of the Home Book of Verse for a friend. If this doesn't seem to be making him feel any better, I add, "—and shoe-trees. They make a bag heavy." Several times I have worked myself up into such a state of sympathy for the man that I have taken one handle of the bag myself. There is one bag in particular that worries

me. It is what the French refer to as a *grande valise* and I don't know what I was thinking of when I bought it. Standing on a station platform it looks like a small rhinoceros crouching for a spring, and I have seen porters run ten feet to one side of it rather than be called upon to lift it.

It holds a great deal more than I have got to put into it, including two small boys, but even with my modest equipment it has to be lifted on and off boats with a crane. There is a story about Louis XVI having hidden his horse in it during the early days of the Revolution, but I rather doubt that, as there would have been no place for the horse to breathe through. However, the fact remains that I don't know what I was thinking of.

Now, this bag is all right when I am abroad, for the porters over there are accustomed to carrying anything up to and including a medium-size garage. They hitch it to a strap with another load the same size on the other end, fling it over their shoulders, perspire freely, and trot off. I would be very glad to feel sorry for them, but they don't seem to mind it at all. It is an older civilization, I guess.

But in the United States I am very uneasy about this bag. I apologize to the porter who puts it on the train and feel that I have to give him enough extra to endow a Negro college in his home town. I start worrying about getting it into a taxi long before the train has pulled into the station, and I run over in my mind a few pleasantries with which I can assuage the porter on the other end. "Pretty heavy, eh? And I don't drink, either! Aha-ha-ha-ha!" or "Maybe I'd better get a trunk, eh?" None of these ever goes very big, I may add.

It usually ends up by my being so self-conscious about the thing that I carry it myself. There are two ways of doing this: one is to carry it by the handles, but that way it crashes heavily against the side of the leg and eventually throws me; the other method is to hoist it up on the shoulder and stagger along under it. This is not much better, for then it not only cocks my hat over my eye but completely shuts off my vision from the other eye, so that many times I have walked head on into another train or collided with passengers. I have even caught up with passengers going in the same direction and smashed into them from behind. And the combined weight of my body and the bag, going at a fair clip, is sufficient to capsize and badly bruise a woman or a small man.

Taxi drivers are not very nice about my bag, either. When confronted with the problem of where to put it in the cab, they often make remarks such as: "Why don't we put the cab on top of the bag and drag it through the streets?" or "Where are the elephants?" With my bag tucked on the front seat beside him, a taxi driver has to lean out over the other side and drive with one knee. And nobody feels sadder about it than I do. Of all people to have a bag like that, I am the worst, because I am so sensitive.

It is not only with railway porters that I am ill at ease. I feel very guilty about asking moving men to carry bureaus and bookcases downstairs. I have a bookcase which I sold to a man three years ago which is still standing in my room because I could not get up courage to ask anyone to move it for me. I know that there are men who make it their business to lift heavy articles of furniture, but this is a *terribly* heavy bookcase. The first six weeks after I sold it I used to sit and look at it and say to myself: "I really ought to get that over to Thurston right away." But I couldn't seem to feel right about getting anyone to do it.

I tried hitching it along the floor myself, but I couldn't even get it away from the spot where it had always been. So then I tried forgetting about it, and would look quickly away every time my eyes rested on it. Thurston asked me about it once, and I said that I had been trying to get a moving man to take it but that there was a strike on. I tried draping it with a sheet, so that I wouldn't have to look at it, but that did no good. The sheet just made it worse.

About a year ago I gave Thurston his money back and said that I had decided to keep the bookcase, but I really don't want it. Perhaps some moving man will see this confession and will come up some day and ask me if I don't want some especially heavy furniture moved. If he *asked* me, I couldn't feel guilty about it, could I? But I can tell him right now that it is heavier than he thinks, and I won't blame him if he drops it on the stairs, and I would rather not watch, if he doesn't mind.

It makes it very difficult to be afraid to impose on porters and yet not to be able to carry things yourself. Perhaps the best thing to do would be just not to own any heavy things, and to buy whatever clothes and shoes I need in the town I happen to be in. Or perhaps it would be better yet not to go anywhere, and just sit in my room.

The Lost Locomotive

THE day that Mr. MacGregor lost the locomotive was a confusing one for our accountants. They didn't know whom to charge it to.

"We have an account here called 'Alterations,'" said the head accountant (Mr. MacGregor). "We might charge it to that. Losing a locomotive is certainly an alteration in something."

"I am afraid that you are whistling in the dark, Mr. MacGregor," I said quietly.

"The point is not what account we are going to charge the lost locomotive to," I continued. "It is how you happened to lose it."

"I have already told you," he replied, with a touch of asperity, "that I haven't the slightest idea. I was tired and nervous and—well—I lost it, that's all!

"As a matter of fact," he snapped, "I am not at all sure that the locomotive is lost. And, if 'It is how you happened to lose it.'"

* * * * *

"I don't think that we need go into that point," I replied. "When a man takes a locomotive out and comes back without it, and is unable to explain what has become of it, the presumption is that he, personally, has lost it. How did you like those tangerines we had for lunch?"

"Only fair," MacGregor answered.

"You see?" I said. "You are getting cynical."

We have had a great deal of trouble about Mr. Mac-Gregor's growing cynical. He looks at things with a bilious eye. It is bringing down the morale of the office force, and there are whole days at a time when we don't sell a thing.

* * * * *

"How often do you take that medicine I gave you?" I asked him.

MacGregor winced slightly. "Hot-diggidy!" he replied.

"That is not an answer to my question," I said, sternly.

"What were we just talking about?" he asked.

"You mean the tangerines?" I said, his cynicism still rankling in my mind.

"No," he replied. "Before that."

We both thought for a minute.

"Well, it couldn't have been very important," I said, laughing. This got him in good humor and we swung forward, double-time, along the road to work.

"Take the Witness!"

NEWSPAPER accounts of trial cross-examinations always bring out the cleverest in me. They induce day dreams in which I am the witness on the stand, and if you don't know some of my imaginary comebacks to an imaginary cross-examiner (Doe vs. Benchley: 482-U.S.-367-398), you have missed some of the most stimulating reading in the history of American jurisprudence.

These little reveries usually take place shortly after I have read the transcript of a trial, while I am on a long taxi ride or seated at a desk with plenty of other work to do. I like them best when I have work to do, as they deplete me mentally so that I am forced to go and lie down after a particularly sharp verbal rally. The knowledge that I have completely floored my adversary, and the imaginary congratulations of my friends (also imaginary), seem more worth while than any amount of fiddling work done.

During these cross-questionings I am always very calm. Calm in a nice way, that is—never cocky. However frantic my inquisitor may wax (and you should see his face at times—it's purple!), I just sit there, burning him up with each answer, winning the admiration of the courtroom and, at times, even a smile from the judge himself. At the end of my examination, the judge is crazy about me.

Just what the trial is about, I never get quite clear

in my mind. Sometimes the subject changes in the middle of the questioning, to allow for the insertion of an especially good crack on my part. I don't think that I am ever actually the defendant, although I don't know why I should feel that I am immune from trial by a jury of my peers—if such exist.

I just sit there, burning him up with each answer

I am usually testifying in behalf of a friend, or perhaps as just an impersonal witness for someone whom I do not know, who, naturally, later becomes my friend for life. It is Justice that I am after—Justice and a few well-spotted laughs.

Let us whip right into the middle of my cross-examination, as I naturally wouldn't want to pull my stuff until I had been insulted by the lawyer, and you can't really get insulted simply by having your name and address asked. I am absolutely fair about these things. If the lawyer will treat me right, I'll treat him right. He has got to start it. For a decent cross-examiner, there is no more tractable witness in the world than I am.

Advancing toward me, with a sneer on his face, he points a finger at me. (I have sometimes thought of pointing my finger back at him, but have discarded that as being too fresh. I don't have to resort to clowning.)

* * * * *

Q—You think you're pretty funny, don't you? (*I have evidently just made some mildly humorous comeback, nothing smart-alecky, but good enough to make him look silly.*)

A—I have never given the matter much thought.

Q—Oh, you haven't given the matter much thought, eh? Well, you seem to be treating this examination as if it were a minstrel show.

A *(very quietly and nicely)*—I have merely been taking my cue from your questions. (*You will notice that all this presupposes quite a barrage of silly questions on his part, and pat answers on mine, omitted here because I haven't thought them up. At any rate, it is evident that I have already got him on the run before this reverie begins.*)

Q—Perhaps you would rather that I conducted this inquiry in baby talk?

A—If it will make it any easier for you. (*Pandemonium, which the Court feels that it has to quell, although enjoying it obviously as much as the spectators.*)

Q *(furious)*—I see. Well, here is a question that I think

53

will be simple enough to elicit an honest answer: Just how did you happen to know that it was eleven-fifteen when you saw the defendant?

A—Because I looked at my watch.

Q—And just why did you look at your watch at this particular time?

A—To see what time it was.

Q—Are you accustomed to looking at your watch often?

A—That is one of the uses to which I often put my watch.

Q—I see. Now, it couldn't by any chance, have been ten-fifteen instead of eleven-fifteen when you looked at your watch this time, could it?

A—Yes, sir. It could.

Q—Oh, it *could* have been ten-fifteen?

A—Yes, sir—if I had been in Chicago. (*Not very good, really. I'll work up something better. I move to have that answer stricken from the record.*)

*   *   *   *   *

When I feel myself lowering my standards by answering like that, I usually give myself a rest, and, unless something else awfully good pops into my head, I adjourn the court until next day. I can always convene it again when I hit my stride.

If possible, however, I like to drag it out until I have really given my antagonist a big final wallop which practically curls him up on the floor (I may think of one before this goes to press), and, wiping his forehead, he mutters, "Take the witness!"

As I step down from the stand, fresh as a daisy, there is a round of applause which the Court makes no attempt to silence. In fact, I have known certain judges to wink pleasantly at me as I take my seat. Judges are only human, after all.

My only fear is that, if I ever really am called upon to testify in court, I won't be asked the right questions. That *would* be a pretty kettle of fish!

The New Strokes

IT WILL be interesting to see what the new season will bring out in the way of novel swimming strokes. I'll bet it involves the use of an auxiliary motor strapped on the shoulders.

When I was learning to swim, people just swam. The idea was to keep afloat and, in an orderly fashion, to get somewhere if possible. If there was nowhere you wanted to get to, you just swam quietly 'round and 'round until your lips got blue. Then you went in.

The stroke that I was first taught was known as the "breast, or gondola, stroke." High out of the water by the bows. It was dignified and stately and went something like this: "One-two-three-sink! One-two-three-sink!" The legs were shot out straight behind, like a frog's, except that they were not good to eat.

* * * * *

Then the more sporting among the swimming crowd took to swimming tipped over on one side, with one ear dragging in the water. This was considered very athletic, especially if one arm was lifted out of the water at each stroke. But even then the procedure was easygoing, pleasant, and more of a pastime than a chore. It was considered very bad form to churn.

But with the advent of the various "crawls," swimming took on more the nature of a battle with the elements. You had to lash at the water, tear at the waves with your teeth, snort and spit, kick your feet like a child with tantrums and, in general, behave as if you

You just swam quietly 'round and 'round

had set out deliberately to drown yourself in an epilepsy. It became tiring just to watch.

*   *   *   *   *

I never learned the names of the new strokes as they came along, but I gather that the instructions for some of them must read:

The Australian Wrench: Place the head under water up to the shoulder blades. Bring the left arm up, over and around the neck until the fingers of the left hand touch the right cheek (still under water). Shove the right arm sideways and to the left until the right shoulder touches the chin. Then shift arm positions suddenly, and with great splashing, propel the body through the water by lashing upward and downward with the feet and legs. The head is kept under water during the entire race, thereby eliminating both wind-resistance and breathing. It is bully fun.

The Navajo Twist: Rotate the entire body like a bobbin on the surface of the water, with elbows and knees bent. Spit while the mouth is on the up-side. Inhale when it is under. This doesn't get you much of anywhere, but it irritates the other swimmers and makes it difficult for them to swim.

The Lighthouse Churn: Just stand still, in water about up to your waist, and beat at the surface with your fists, snorting and spitting at the same time. This does nothing but make you conspicuous, but, after all, what is modern swimming for?

Fun with Animals

THE news that a small, blackfoot penguin in the New York Aquarium had sprained its ankle when it stepped on a marshmallow served only to remind us that no one of God's creatures, however smart, is immune from loss of dignity. No one is infallible.

If anyone ought to be able to walk along without slipping, it is a penguin. Accustomed to treading the slippery surfaces of the globe with considerable assurance, if not manner, the penguin is one animal from whom you would expect accurate footwork.

And yet one small marshmallow, undoubtedly left there by an admirer, threw this penguin to the tune of a sprained ankle.

I worked on a motion picture once with a penguin named Eddie. Eddie put on quite a lot of airs for himself as a stroller, but I never saw him walk ten feet without tripping over a cable or something, and tripping rather badly, too. When Eddie tripped, he fell, and fell heavily, but he was always up again in a thrice, pretending that he had just been clowning.

There is a great satisfaction to us clumsy humans when we see an animal that is supposed to surpass us in skill making a monkey of itself.

* * * * *

I am still gloating over a blackbird that I saw, with

my own eyes, in as disgraceful a bit of flying as any novice ever put on.

I was sitting in an automobile by the side of the curb when this bird swooped down. With some idea, evidently, of making a two-point landing, just to show off. Well, just as his feet hit the sidewalk, one of them slipped out from under him, and I was a witness to the remarkable sight of a full-grown, adult bird falling on its tail. A vaudeville comic couldn't have taken a neater spill.

The chagrin and humiliation of that blackbird were gratifying to see. He got back his balance immediately and tried to act as if nothing had happened, but he knew that I had seen him and he was furious. He was off in the air again right away, but not before I had sneered: "Nyaya!" at him and called "Get a horse!"

Everyone ought to see a bird slip on its tail at least once. It is a gratifying experience and one good for the soul.

The Truth
About Thunderstorms

ONE of the advantages of growing older and putting
on weight is that a man can admit to being afraid
of certain things which, as a stripling, he had to face
without blanching. I will come right out and say that I
mean thunderstorms.

For years I have been concealing my nervousness during thunderstorms, or, at least, I have flattered myself
that I was concealing it. I have scoffed at women who
gave signs of being petrified, saying, "Come, come!
What is there to be afraid of?" And all the time I *knew*
what there was to be afraid of, and that it was a good,
crashing sock on the head with a bolt of lightning.
People *do* get it, and I have no particular reason for believing that I am immune. On the contrary.

Just where any of us in the human race get off to
adopt the Big-Man attitude of "What is there to be
afraid of?" toward lightning is more than I can figure
out. You would think that we knew what lightning is.
You would think that we knew how to stop it. You
would think that no one but women and yellow dogs
were ever hit by it and that no man in a turtle-neck
sweater and a three days' beard on his chin would give
it a second thought. I am sick of all this bravado about
lightning and am definitely abandoning it herewith.

Ever since I was a child old enough to have any pride in the matter I have been wincing inwardly whenever 100,000 volts of simon-pure electricity cut loose in the air. My nervous system has about six hundred ingrowing winces stored up inside it, and that is bad for any nervous system. From now on I am going to humor mine and give a shrill scream whenever I feel like it, and that will be whenever there is a good sharp flash of lightning. I will say this for myself: I will scream when the lightning flashes and not when the thunder sounds. I may be timid but I am no fool.

My nervousness begins when I see the black clouds in the distance. At the sound of the first rumble my digestive system lays off work, leaving whatever odds and ends of assimilation there may be until later in the day.

Of course, up until now I have never allowed myself to show trepidation. If I happened to be out on the water or playing tennis when it was evident that a storm was coming, I have looked casually at my watch and said, "Ho-hum! What about going in and making a nice, cool drink?" Sometimes I even come right out and say, "It looks like a storm—we'd better get in"; but there is always some phlegmatic guy who says, "Oh, we aren't going to get that—it's going around the mountain," and, by the time it is evident that we *are* going to get that and it *isn't* going around the mountain, it is too late.

It is remarkable how slow some people can be in taking down a tennis net or bringing a boat inshore when there is a thunderstorm on the way. They must not only take the net down but they must fold it up, very carefully and neatly, or they must put things away all shipshape in the cabin and coil ropes. Anything to waste time.

My attempts to saunter toward the house on such occasions must have, at times, given away the dread I have of being the recipient of a bolt of lightning. I guess that I have done some of the fastest sauntering ever pulled off on a dry track. Especially if my arms are loaded down with cushions and beach umbrellas I make a rather ungainly job of trying to walk as if I didn't care and yet make good time.

If possible, I usually suggest that someone run ahead

and shut the windows in the house, and then immediately delegate myself to this job. I am not so crazy about shutting windows during a thunderstorm, but it is better than dawdling around outside.

I once got caught up in an airplane during an electrical storm. In fact, there were *two* storms, one on the right and one on the left, and we were heading right for the spot where they were coming together. We could see them quite a long time before they hit us, and I was full of good suggestions which the pilot didn't take. I wanted to put down right where we were. It was a rocky country, covered with scrub pines, but it seemed to be preferable to hanging around up in the air.

I was considerably reassured, however, by being told (or shouted to) that you are safer up in the air during a thunderstorm than you are on the earth, as lightning cannot strike unless the object is "grounded." It sounded logical to me, or as logical as anything connected with lightning ever could sound, and I sat back to enjoy my first electrical display in comfort. It really was great, although I hate to admit it. You couldn't hear the thunder because of the motors and there were some very pretty flashes.

It was only several months after, on reading of a plane being struck by lightning three thousand feet up, that I began to get nervous. Perhaps you can't get hit unless you are "grounded," according to all the laws of nature, but it is always the exception that proves the rule, and it would be just my luck to be one of the exceptions.

Perhaps the worst part that a nervous man has to play during a crisis like this is reassuring the ladies. If I am alone, I can give in and go down cellar, but when there are women around I have to be brave and joke and yell "Bang!" every time there is a crash. To make matters worse, I find that there are a great many women who are not frightened, and who want to sit out on the porch and play bridge through the whole thing.

This is a pretty tough spot for a man of my temperament. At best, I am an indifferent bridge player, even with the sun shining or a balmy summer night's breeze wafting around outside. I have to go very carefully with my bidding and listen to everything that is being said or I am in danger of getting a knife in my back from my

partner when the game is over. But with a thunderstorm raging around my ears and trees crashing down in the yard by my elbow, I might just as well be playing "slap-jack" for all the sense I make.

A good flash of lightning has been known to jolt a "Five spades" out of me, with an eight and queen of spades in my hand. Sometimes it would almost have been better if the bolt had hit me. (Only fooling, Lord! Just kidding!)

I would feel more ashamed of confessing all this if I weren't sure that I am in the right about it. I am not afraid of snakes or burglars or ghosts or even Mussolini, but when it comes to lightning—boy, there's something to be afraid *of!* And anyone who says that he isn't is either lying or an awful sap.

Of course, being nervous isn't going to keep you from getting hit, but when you are nervous you don't lie around with water dripping on you and holding a copper plate in your mouth, and avoiding all this sort of thing certainly helps.

If I were running a thunderstorm I would pick out some big man who goes around saying there is nothing to be afraid of and clip a cigar or two out from between his teeth just to show him. And any nice guy like me, who knows his place and tries to keep it, I would let go scot-free and might even uproot a fine big pot of buried gold pieces for him.

The funny part about all this is that now that I am old enough to come out frankly and admit how I feel about thunderstorms, I seem to be getting too old to mind them so much. It has been a couple of years now since I had a really good scare (I am now knocking wood so hard that the man in the next room just yelled "Come in!"). Perhaps it is just that, when you get to be my age, it doesn't make so much difference. If it isn't lightning, it will be hardening of the arteries. I still would prefer hardening of the arteries, however.

Rapping the Wrapper!

PROGRESS is all right in its way and I suppose that, if you have progressed as far as you feel you can in one line, it is permissible to try progressing in another. (I can't get arrested for saying *that*, certainly.)

It broke into a hundred bits in the middle

There used to be an advertisement which read: "We couldn't improve the product, so we improved the wrapper." That's fine, provided you *do* improve the wrapper. But there is such a thing as improving the wrapper so that nobody can get at the product. It may be a perfectly dandy wrapper, air-tight, water-tight and

67

germ-proof, but if the buyer has to send it to a garage to get it off, something is wrong somewhere.

I have just been trying to get at a roll of mints. I bought them at a newsstand thinking that I would slip one of them into my mouth before meeting my wife.

I turned it over and started on the other

So I started clawing at the end with one nail as I walked along. It was obviously not the end to claw at. So I turned it over and started on the other. That end had been clamped down by a stamping machine usually reserved for tinning sardines. I tried biting at both ends (one after the other, naturally) and gave up just before an inlay came out.

Now all that I wanted was a mint, mind you. If I had wanted to uncrate a piano or crack a safe I would have expected to go to some trouble. But when all a man wants is a mint just before he meets his wife, the least that he can ask is that the mint will go half way with him. These mints were out-and-out antagonistic.

I finally saw that it was a personal matter, and gave my whole attention to it. If it was a fight they wanted, I was game. I stopped short on the sidewalk and laid my hat over a hydrant. I tried breaking the thing over my knee and hitting it against a building. (Round One. The mints.)

It finally ended by my dashing the whole business to the sidewalk as a child does a torpedo, with the result that it broke into a hundred bits. It broke into a hundred bits in the middle, but the two ends remained intact and as tightly clamped down as they had been when they left the foundry.

Now I don't have to have mints. It should be a case of you-treat-me-right-and-I'll-treat-you-right between me and the manufacturers. If it isn't going to be, I have other resources.

Good Bison News

A VERY comforting fact was just called to my attention concerning bison, and I think that every comforting fact ought to be passed on these days. The bison of America are not, as we have always been led to believe, on the verge of extinction. On the contrary, the work for their conservation has been so successful that there are now too many bison.

All this has probably been common gossip among bison-fanciers for many months, but I have been out in the Far West where they don't go in much for this Nature business, and it was not until I returned to New York that I learned definitely that all was well with the American buffalo. In fact, the problem now is: "What to do with the extra ones?"

The last I heard about these shaggy beasts there were only a few of them left and those were dying off like flies. "Isn't it too bad about the bison?" everyone was saying, gloomily. "In ten years there won't be one left." Then the war came, and people got to thinking about other things, and, if you had come up to me last week and asked me if I wanted to see a bison I should have said: "Don't be silly! There are no more."

But very quietly for twenty-five years the American Bison Society has been working tooth and nail to save this noble breed of typical American animal, and they have done so well at their work that last year 1,400 surplus bison had to be killed. It would almost seem that they had overshot their mark.

Just how you would go about saving buffaloes from extinction I do not know, but, whatever the secret was, the American Bison Society certainly hit upon it. I suppose that the bison themselves had something to do with it, but they evidently hadn't quite got the knack of the thing before the American Bison Society came along.

The President of the Society is as much at sea as anyone else. "When we began conserving these animals," he is quoted as saying, "every one believed they would become extinct within a few years. It was simply a gesture on our part to keep alive as long as possible a memory of the Old West. But the buffalo did not die, as you see, and our problem now has become one of getting enough food and space for him."

It may have been just a gesture on the part of the American Bison Society, but it was a gesture that packed a punch. Evidently the bison took it seriously. Old West or New West, it is now fixed for bison for many years to come. In Canada alone last year there were 6,300 buffaloes, which was exactly 1,200 too many for the available standing space. Somebody has got to speak to them, in private, and tell them that a joke is a joke.

The thing goes more or less in a circle, for the income from the hides and meat of the bison, which have to be killed to make room for the others, is used to provide food for the newcomers and their Indian caretakers. But it is rather a tough fate for a member of a proud breed, who thought he was being saved from extinction, to find himself being slaughtered to make

6

room for others coming in. He might even ask, with perfect justice: "What is this—a gag?" It might almost have been more fun to have been a member of a rapidly disappearing species than to be hustled into an abattoir as "surplus stock."

But the memory of the Old West is in no danger of dying out, as far as bison are concerned, at any rate. And the American Bison Society has proved what can be done by putting your mind to it. The President says that all other big game are also increasing, with the exception of the mountain sheep. "I'm afraid his kind will be gone in a few years despite what we can do," he adds, sadly.

Fie! Those are defeatist words! What was done for the bison ought to be able to be done for the mountain sheep. Only this time it might be well to establish a quota.

Back in Line

FOR a nation which has an almost evil reputation for bustle, bustle, bustle, and rush, rush, rush, we spend an enormous amount of time standing around in line in front of windows, just waiting. It would be all right if we were Spanish peasants and could strum guitars and hum, or even stab each other, while we were standing in line, or East Indians who could just sit cross-legged and simply stare into space for hours. Nobody expects anything more of Spanish peasants or East Indians, because they have been smart enough to build themselves a reputation for picturesque lethargy.

But we in America have built ourselves reputations for speed and dash, and are known far and wide as the rushingest nation in the world. So when fifty of us get in a line and stand for an hour shifting from one foot to the other, rereading the shipping news and cooking recipes in an old newspaper until our turn comes, we just make ourselves look silly.

Most of this line-standing is the fault of the Government, just as everything else which is bad in our national life is the fault of the Government, including stone bruises and tight shoes. We would have plenty of time to rush around as we are supposed to do, if the Government did not require 500 of us to stand in one line at once waiting for two civil service employees to weigh our letters, thumb out income-tax blanks, tear off our customs slips or roll back our eyelids. Of course, there are times when we stand in line to see a ball game or buy a railroad ticket, but that is *our* affair, and in time we get enough sense to stop going to ball games or traveling on railroads.

The U. S. Post Office is one of the most popular line-standing fields in the country. It has been estimated that six-tenths of the population of the United States spend their entire lives standing in line in a post office. When you realize that no provision is made for their eating or sleeping or intellectual advancement while they are thus standing in line, you will understand why six-tenths of the population look so cross and peaked. The wonder is that they have the courage to go on living at all.

This congestion in the post offices is due to what are technically known as "regulations" but what are really a series of acrostics and anagrams devised by some officials who got around a table one night and tried to be funny. "Here's a good gag!" one of them probably cried. "Let's make it so that as soon as a customer reaches the window with his package after his forty-five minutes in line, he has to go home again, touch some object made of wood, turn around three times, and then come back and stand in line again!" "No, no, that's too easy!" another objected. "Let's make it compulsory for the package to be wrapped in paper which is water-marked with Napoleon's coat of arms. We won't say anything about it until they get right up to the window, so there will be no danger of their bringing that kind of paper with them. Then they will have to go away again with their bundles, find some paper water-marked with Napoleon's coat of arms (of which there is none that I ever heard of), rewrap their bundles, and come back and stand in line again. What do you say to that!" This scheme probably threw the little group of officials into such a gale of merriment that they had to call the meeting off and send down for some more White Rock.

You can't tell me that the post-office regulations (to say nothing of those of the Custom House and Income Tax Bureau) were made with anything else in mind except general confusion. It must be a source of great chagrin to those in charge to think of so many people being able to stick a stamp on a letter and drop it into a mail box without any trouble or suffering at all. They are probably working on that problem at this very minute, trying to devise some way in which the public can be made to fill out a blank, stand in line, consult some underling who will refer them to a superior, and then be made to black up with burned cork before they can mail a letter. And they'll figure it out, too. They always have.

But at present their chief source of amusement is in torturing those unfortunates who find themselves with a package to send by mail. And with Christmas in the offing, they must be licking their chops with glee in very anticipation. Although bundles of old unpaid bills are about all anyone will be sending this Christmas, it doesn't make any difference to the P. O. Department. A package is a package, and you must suffer for it.

It wouldn't be a bad idea for those of us who have been through the fire to get together and cheat the officials out of their fun this year by sending out lists of instructions (based on our own experience) to all our friends, telling them just what they have got to look out for before they start to stand in line. Can you imagine the expression on the face of a post-office clerk if a whole line of people came up to his window, one by one, each with his package so correctly done up that there was no fault to find with it? He would probably shoot himself in the end, rather than face his superiors with the confession that he had sent no one home to do the whole thing over. And if his superiors shot themselves too it would not detract one whit from the joyousness of the Christmas tide.

So here are the things I have learned in my various visits to the post office. If you will send me yours and get ten friends to make a round robin of their experiences, we may thwart the old Government yet.

Packages to be mailed abroad must be:

1. Wrapped in small separate packages, each weighing no more than one pound and seven-eighths (Eastern

Standard Time), and each package to be tied with blue ribbon in a sheepshank knot. (Any sailor of fifteen years' experience will teach you to tie a sheepshank.)

2. The address must be picked out in blue, and reënforced with an insertion of blue ribbon, no narrower than three-eighths of an inch and no wider than five-eighths of an inch, and certainly not exactly four-eighths or one-half, or else you may have to stay and write it out a hundred times after the post office has closed.

3. The package, no matter what size, will have to be made smaller.

4. The package, no matter what size, will have to be made larger.

(In order to thwart the clerk on these last two points, it will be necessary to have packages of *all* sizes concealed in a bag slung over your back.)

5. The person who is mailing the package must approach the window with the package held in his right hand, extended toward the clerk one foot from the body, while with the left hand he must carry a small bunch of lilies of the valley, with a tag on them reading: "Love from—[name of sender]—to the U. S. Post Office."

6. The following ritual will then be adhered to, a deviation by a single word subjecting the sender to a year in Leavenworth or both:

Clerk's Question: Do you want to mail a package?

Sender's Answer: No, sir.

Q. What *do* you want to do?

A. I don't much care, so long as I can be with you.

Q. Do you like tick-tack-toe?

A. I'm crazy mad for it.

77

Q. Very well. We won't play that.

A. Aren't you being just a little bit petty?

Q. Aren't you criticizing *me*?

A. Sorry.

Q. And high time. Now what do you want?

A. *You*, dear.

Q. You get along with yourself. What's in your hand?

A. Flowers for you—*dear*.

Q. I know that. What's in the other hand?

A. I won't tell.

Q. Give it here this minute.

A. You won't like it.

Q. Give-it-here-this-minute, I say.

The sender reluctantly gives over the parcel.

Q. What do you want to do with this?

A. I want to take it home with me and wrap it up again.

Q. You leave it here, and *like it*.

A. Please give it back. Please, pretty please?

Q. I will do no such thing. You leave it here and I will mail it for you. And shut up!

The sender leaves the window, sobbing. The clerk, just to be mean, mails the package.

The Chinese Situation

With "The Good Pulitzer Earth" being made into both a movie and a play (which means six imitations in each field if it proves successful), to say nothing of Mrs. Pearl Buck's going right ahead and bringing descendants of old Wang into the publishing world, just as if there were plenty of food to go around, it looks as if we were in for a good, old-fashioned Chinese winter.

Before the thing has gone too far (which it will), let us see just how far it can go. EDITOR'S NOTE: Owing to the subsequent failure of the play and the postponement of the movie until next year, it went no further than the following parody.

IT WAS the birthday of Whang the Gong. Whang the Gong was the son of Whang the Old Man, and the brother of Whang the Rich and of Auld Whang Syne. He was very poor and had only the tops of old Chinese wives to eat, but in his soul he was very proud and in his heart he knew that he was the son of old Whang Lung who had won the Pulitzer Prize for the Hop-Sing-and-Jump.

Now Whang the Gong, although he was known far and wide among the local missionaries as a heathen, had read enough of the Gospels to know the value of short words and the effectiveness of the use of the word "and." And so Whang the Gong spoke, and it was good. Good for fifty cents a word.

Now Whang the Gong awoke on the morning of his birthday, and opened one eye, and it was not good, so he shut it again. And he opened the other eye, and it was worse than the first. So the young man shook his head willfully and said: "I will open no more eyes until the harvest comes." Now the harvest was full six months away, which gave the young man a hell of a lot of leeway, and he rolled over again and slept.

But Rum Blossom, the wife of Whang the Gong, did not sleep. At four in the morning, before even the kine had begun to low or the water to run in the tub, Rum Blossom had rubbed her small hand over her small eyes, and it was not good. It was lousy. She arose, then, and went into the pump-house.

"Excuse," she said to nobody in particular, as nobody in particular was listening to her words, "excuse—I am going to have a baby." So she went into the pump-house, and, while the waffles were cooking, she had a baby, and it was a man. Which was pretty good, when you consider that it was born between waffles.

Now the winter wore on, and it was still the birthday of Whang the Gong, for Whang the Gong liked birthdays, for birthdays are holidays and holidays are good. And Rum Blossom, his wife, came to him and said, lowering her eyes as she pulled the stump of an old tree and threw it into the wood-box, "I am going to have another baby." And Whang the Gong said: "That is up to you." And he rolled over and shut another eye, which was his third, kept especially for shutting.

So Rum Blossom went into the library and had another baby. And it was a woman, or slave, baby, which, in China, is not so hot.

"I will scream your shame to the whole village," said Whang the Gong when he had heard of the incident. "Yesterday you had a man child, which was good. Today you have a girl, which is bitterness upon my head and the taste of aloes in my mouth." And he repeated it over and over, such being the biblical style, "I will tell the village—I will tell the village." And Rum Blossom, his wife, said: "All right. Go ahead and tell the village. Only get up out of bed, at any rate. And get your old man up out of bed, too. I am sick of seeing him around, doing nothing."

And Whang the Gong got up out of his bed, and got his Old Man up out of his bed, all of which made but little difference.

He went without reply then to the wall and felt for the roughness which was the mark of his clothes-closet, and he removed the clod of earth which fastened it. "I will have my cutaway," he said, and went then back to bed. And Rum Blossom his wife came to him and said:

"I will get you your cutaway just as soon as I have had a child," and going into the clothes-closet, she had a child and came out with the cutaway. "Here," she said, "is your cutaway. Take it and like it." And Whang the Gong took it, and liked it, for it was a good cutaway.

It seemed as though once the gods turn against a man they will not consider him again. The rains, which should have come in the early summer, withheld themselves until the fifteenth of October, which was the date for Rum Blossom to have another baby.

And Whang the Gong said to Whang Lung, the old man his father, "How come? We have no rain." And Whang the Old Man said, "True, you have no rain. But you have babies galore. One may not ask everything."

And Whang the Gong was stumped. "A baby is but a baby," he said in confusion. "But rain is rain." All of which made no sense, but sounded good.

But the Old Man would hear none of his son's sophistry, and mouthed his gums, which were of tutti-frutti, and rolled in the grass, only there was no grass and so the Old Man rolled in the stones and bruised himself quite badly. But all this meant nothing to Whang the Gong, for three moons had passed since he had eaten nothing but spinach and his eyes were on those of Lettuce, the Coat Room Girl.

There was a day when Whang the Gong awoke and saw his wife, Rum Blossom, pacing up and down the room but, as the room was only three paces long, the effect was unimpressive.

"Another baby, I suppose?" said Whang the Gong, shutting both eyes.

"Not so that you could notice it," replied his wife, in extremest pique. "I'm through." And there was that in her pique which allowed no come-back, and Whang the Gong knew that she was indeed through, which was O.K. with him.

And when pay-day came, Whang the Gong arose and put on his finest silken suit with an extra pair of pants

82

and married Lettuce the Coat Room Girl, making two wives for Whang the Gong, one, Rum Blossom, to keep the books, and one, Lettuce the Coat Room Girl, to be the mother of his children. Which made it very simple, so simple that every one watching, smiled.

Nature's Prizes

AS SOME Frenchman has said, translating at sight into English as he went: "Each one to his taste"; but, with all the things there are to go out after in the world, I think that Dr. Ditmars is going out after the least attractive. At least, they would be to me.

Dr. Ditmars, head of The Bronx Zoo, is going on an expedition to the Caribbean Sea, and, believe it or not, he is hoping and praying that he comes back with the following treasures:

One Surinam toad, which, according to Dr. Ditmars, "looks as if an elephant had stepped on it, and has small beady eyes, like pin-points." This is all right, I suppose, so long as Dr. Ditmars thinks he wants it.

One Giant Horned Frog which attains a length of more than ten inches. "It is bright green, has long yellow horns, barks like a dog, and can inflict a very severe bite. It is apt to jump at you and bite you with no warning whatever." Not at *me*, Dr. Ditmars, not at *me*. He couldn't jump that far.

One tropical spider or *Grammostola lomgimanca*, which is three times as large as the common tarantula. In addition to being very active, this spider is also very poisonous, and its bite may have a fatal result.

One tree frog of the Harlequin family, highly colored. "Their skins exude a poison which is used by Indians in northeastern South America to tip their arrows. The venom is said to be as deadly as strychnine if it enters the bloodstream, and is fatal within ten minutes."

* * * * *

Now Dr. Ditmars aim is not to keep as far away from these pets as possible, but actually to go out and *get* them. He wants to bring them back to The Bronx Zoo, although, so far, no residents of The Bronx have issued statements in the matter. It looks like a good year for house screens in The Bronx.

The only one of Dr. Ditmars' quarries which could hold my attention at all is the Surinam toad "which looks as if an elephant had stepped on it." I'd rather like to look at that, and then look right away again.

The Surinam toad also has quite a cute trick in disposing of its eggs. (All this is, of course, according to Dr. Ditmars. It comes like a bolt from the blue to me.) The female lays the eggs in the water, each egg floating by itself. The male then takes them, one by one, in his flipper and imbeds them in the back of the female, where a retaining membrane immediately forms. The young frogs remain on this refuge until they can take care of themselves. More than two hundred eggs have been found on the back of a single female.

* * * * *

Well, as the Frenchman said, "Each one to his taste." I couldn't go for that sort of thing myself—but then, I couldn't go for any of the other of Dr. Ditmars' hobbies.

One Minute, Please

ABOUT an hour ago the telephone bell rang. I answered it after a fashion.

A very brisk young woman said, "Wait a minute, please," but she didn't mean the "please." What she obviously meant was just "Wait a minute!"

Now this is a thing that especially irks me. When I am called by a secretary who doesn't tell me who is calling, but says, "Wait a minute" and then goes off somewhere for five minutes, I hang up.

So I hung up. "They'll call back," I said to myself, and stood waiting by the instrument.

I tried to read the paper I had in my hand, but couldn't concentrate. Each second I could hear that bell ringing, only it didn't ring. I sat down by the telephone. "There's no sense in going back into the room," I thought. "It'll come any minute now." But it didn't.

* * * * *

The sound of a telephone bell which ought to ring any minute, but doesn't, is much worse than the actual thing. By this time I was definitely on edge. I was also in a frenzy to know who the caller had been.

Finally I went into the other room. "That'll bring them," I said to myself, sagely. I know how those things work.

86

But I overestimated their perversity this time. Even when I sat down in a low, easy chair, difficult to get out of, it didn't work. As a final ruse I lay down on a couch and pretended to be asleep. No bell.

I couldn't concentrate

I thought of calling Central and asking who had called me, but that would be weak. Anyway, Central couldn't tell me. I thought of calling all my friends and asking them if they had just called, but that would be pretty futile on the face of it. I thought of putting the whole matter out of my mind, but that was impossible. I was obsessed.

*   *   *   *   *

It has been an hour now and I have been pacing up and down the room gnawing at my nails. Obviously whoever it was is *not* going to call back. In a weak attempt to restore my peace of mind I am using this space as a

PERSONAL COLUMN

At five-thirty on the afternoon of Tuesday,
June 25, *who called me on the telephone?*

Filling That Hiatus

THERE has already been enough advice written for hostesses and guests so that there should be no danger of toppling over forward into the wrong soup or getting into arguments as to which elbow belongs on which arm. The etiquette books have taken care of all that.

There is just one little detail of behavior at dinner parties which I have never seen touched upon, and which has given me personally some little embarrassment. I refer to the question of what to do during those little intervals when you find that both your right-hand and your left-hand partner are busily engaged in conversation with somebody else.

You have perhaps turned from what you felt to be a fascinating conversation (on your part) with your right-hand partner, turned only to snap away a rose bug which was charging on your butter from the table decorations or to refuse a helping of salad descending on you from the left, and when you turn back to your partner to continue your monologue, you find that she is already vivaciously engaged on the other side, a shift made with suspicious alacrity, when you come to think it over. So you wheel about to your left, only to find yourself confronted by the clasp of a necklace and an expanse of sun-browned back. This leaves you looking more or less straight in front of you, with a roll in your hand and not very much to do with your face. Should you sit and cry softly to yourself, with your underlip stuck out and tears coursing unnoticed down your cheeks, or should you launch forth into a bawdy solo, beating time with your knife and fork?

Of course, the main thing is not to let your hostess notice that you are disengaged, for, if she spots you dawdling or looking into space, she will either think that you have insulted both your partners or else will feel responsible for you herself and start a long-distance conversation which has no real basis except that of emergency. So above all things you must spend the hiatus acting as if you really were doing something.

You can always make believe that you are talking to the person opposite

You can always make believe that you are talking to the person opposite, making little conversational faces and sounds into thin air, nodding your head "Yes" or "No," and laughing politely every now and again, perhaps even continuing the talk from which you had been cut off, just as if someone were still listening to you. This may fool your hostess in case her glance happens to fall your way (and sometime we must take up the difficulty of talking to hostesses whose glances must, of necessity, be roving up and down the board while you are trying to be funny) but it is going to confuse the person sitting opposite you in case he or she happens to catch your act. If one looks across the table and sees the man opposite laughing and talking straight ahead with nobody on the other end, one is naturally going to think that he had better not take any more to drink, or perhaps even that he had better not go out to any more parties until some good specialist has gone over him thoroughly. It is this danger of being misjudged which makes the imitation conversation inadvisable.

You can always get busily at work on the nuts in front of your plate, arranging them on the tablecloth in fancy patterns with simulated intensity which will make it look as if you were performing for somebody's benefit, especially if you keep looking up at an imaginary audience and smiling "See?" Even if you are caught at this, there is no way of checking up, for anyone of the dinner guests might possibly be looking at you while talking to somebody else. It isn't much fun, however, after the first five minutes.

If you have thought to bring along a bit of charcoal, you can draw little pictures on the back on either side of you, or lacking charcoal and the ability to draw, you might start smothering the nicer-looking back with kisses. This would, at least, get one of your partners to turn around—unless she happened to like it. As time wears on, and you still find yourself without anyone to talk to, you can start juggling your cutlery, beginning with a knife, fork, and spoon and working up to two of each, with perhaps a flower thrown in to make it harder. This ought to attract *some* attention.

Of course, there is always one last resort, and that is to slide quietly out of your chair and under the table,

You can draw little pictures

where you can either crawl about collecting slippers which have been kicked off, growling like a dog and frightening the more timid guests, or crawl out from the other side and go home. Perhaps this last would be best.

What Are Little Boys
Made of?

DID you know that you have enough resin in your system to rub up a hundred violin A strings? Or enough linoleum to carpet two medium-sized rooms (without bath)? You were probably not aware of these valuable properties lying dormant in your physical make-up and yet scientists tell us that they are there.

As you all were taught in school, our body is made up of millions and millions of tiny particles called the Solar System. These tiny particles are called 'aeons," and it would take one of them fifteen million years to reach the sun if it ever broke loose and *wanted* to get to the sun.

Well, anyway, these millions and millions of tiny particles are composed of hydrogen, oxygen, iodine, phosphorus, Rhode Island, Connecticut. There is also a blue-plate dinner for those who don't like iodine. The action of all these elements sets up a ferment (C_2HN_4, or common table pepper) which sometimes ends in digestion but more often does not. If any one of these agents is lacking in our make-up, due to our having dressed in a hurry, we say we are "deficient," or perhaps we "feel awful." Even with everything working I don't feel so hot.

It is only recently that doctors have discovered that

we have many more elements in our systems than was originally thought. Whether we have always had them and just didn't know it, or whether they were brought there and left by some people who wanted to get rid of them has not been decided.

They tell us that the average 150-pound body (and a very pretty way to phrase it, too) contains enough carbon alone to make 9,000 lead pencils (not one of them ever sharpened, probably).

Another item which the doctors tell us we have in abundance is hydrogen—"enough in excess," they put it, "to fill about a hundred child's balloons." There's a pretty picture for you! As if we didn't have troubles enough as it is, we must go about with the consciousness that we have the makings of one hundred child's balloons inside us, and that under the right conditions we might float right off our chairs and bounce against the ceiling until pulled down by friends!

Thinking of ourselves in terms of balloons, lead pencils, whitewash (we have enough lime in us to whitewash a chicken coop, says one expert), and matches (we are fools to bother with those little paper books of matches, for we are carrying around enough phosphorus to make 2,200 match heads), all this rather makes a mockery of dressing up in evening clothes or brushing our hair. We might just as well get a good big truck and pile ourselves into it in the raw whenever we want to go anywhere, with perhaps some good burlap bags to keep the rain off. There is no sense in trying to look nice when all that is needed is a sandwich-board sign reading: "Anything on this counter—15 cents."

And that is the ultimate insult that these inventory

We might float right off our chairs

hounds have offered us: they tell us just how much all this truck of which we are made is worth in dollars and cents. They didn't have to do that. Put all our bones, brains, muscles, nerves, and everything that goes into the composition of our bodies onto scales and, at the current market prices, the whole lot would bring just a little over a dollar. This is on the hoof, mind you. If you wanted to tie each element up in little packages with Japanese paper and ribbon, or if we went to the trouble to weather them up a bit and call them antiques, we might be able to ask a little more.

For example, the average body, such as might meet another body comin' through the rye, contains only about one-tenth of a drop of tincture of iodine at any one time, and one-tenth of a drop would hardly be worth the dropper to pick it up for the retail trade. And yet, if we *don't* have that tenth of a drop something happens to our thyroid gland and we sit around the village grocery store all days saying "Nyaya!" Or to our pituitary gland and we end up wearing a red coat in a circus, billed as Walter, the Cardiff Behemoth: Twice the Size of an Ordinary Man and Only Half as Bright.

I don't see why scientists couldn't have let us alone and not told us about this. There was a day when I could bounce out of bed with the lark (I sometimes let the lark get out first, just to shut the window and turn on the heat, but I wasn't far behind), plunge into a cold tub (with just a dash of warm to take off the chill), eat a hearty breakfast, and be off to work with a light heart.

But now I get out of bed very carefully, if at all, thinking of those 9,000 lead pencils which are inside me. Too much water seems to be a risk, with all that iron lying around loose. Exercise is out of the question when you consider 2,200 match heads which might jolt up against each other and start a very pretty blaze before you were halfway to work.

Suppose that we *are* as full of knicknacks as the doctors say. Why not let the whole matter drop and just forget about it? Now that they have put the thing into our heads, the only way to get it out is for some expert to issue a statement saying that everyone has been mistaken and that what we really are made of is a solid mechanism of unrustable cast iron and if anything goes wrong, just have a man come up from the garage and look it over.

Elevator Weather

TALKING about the weather is all very well if you are among friends and don't let the talk get rough, but it does seem as if we ought to draw the line somewhere. (Of course, this is only my personal opinion and I may be old-fashioned, but I would rather be old-fashioned than terribly terribly ill with fever and have to wear ice-packs for weeks on end.)

I do think that we talk about the weather with a lot of people who don't know anything about it. For example (and it is the only one that I can think of at the moment), elevator-men. If there is one class of workers who are asked questions about the weather from morning until night it is the elevator-men. And if there is one class which knows absolutely nothing about the weather, it is also elevator-men. Let us see if this is not true.

The elevator-man shall we say, gets into his elevator at eight o'clock in the morning. Unless he happens to be running the elevator in the Eiffel Tower or some other openwork structure he never sees the daylight again until he goes out to lunch. Next to stokers in an ocean liner there are no workers who have less opportunity to form an opinion on the weather. A tornado could appear on the horizon and sweep across town in a leisurely manner and disappear on the opposite horizon, and the elevator-man would never know—unless it happened to rip his building down.

And yet we come in from the outside, with an abundant supply of red-hot information on the subject, and the first thing we say to the elevator-man is: "What is it going to do—rain?"

And the elevator-man, either to humor us or because he feels himself to have some strange intuitive sense, replies: "It certainly looks like it."

If one wanted to heckle and be nasty, one might come back with: "*What* looks like it?" This would force him into an admission that he was basing his judgment on the appearance of the twelfth, fourteenth, and fifteenth floors as he shot past them. But that would be hardly fair to do, as we ourselves brought the matter up and led him into committing himself.

Did you ever stop to think that every person who gets into an elevator and finds himself alone with the operator makes some comment or asks some question concerning the weather outside? Did you ever stop to think what that means to the elevator-man? From eight until six he has no conversation addressed to him except that dealing with heat or cold, rain or shine.

On the first warm spring day, along about four in the afternoon, an elevator-man told me that he had said: "It certainly does!" just three hundred and twelve times in answer to people coming in from the outside and saying: "Well, it looks as if spring were here!"

"I am often tempted to deny it, sir," he said, with a wan look in his eye. "I am often tempted when they come out with 'Well, it looks as if spring were here,' to snap back at them and say: 'Oh, you think so, do you? or 'That just shows all you know about it.' But what would be the good, sir? It would only confuse them, and there we should be."

"What is it going to do—rain?"

I do feel, however, that something ought to be done, either to stop people from asking the elevator-man what the weather is going to be, or to keep him from answering as if he really knew. It is almost hopeless to keep people from asking. That is more of a reflex action on their parts, like twitching. One enters an elevator and one asks the man whether or not it is going to rain. It is purely physiological reaction, just as one winces slightly before entering a subway turnstile or ducks when going under the Brooklyn Bridge on a Fall River boat. There is no sense in starting a campaign to keep people from asking the elevator-man about the weather. The only thing to do is to discourage elevator-men from answering.

My plan would be this: Select a company of perhaps eight men to go about town from elevator to elevator. They assemble outside the building and run over their lines. The first one enters the elevator alone.

"Is it going to rain?" he asks the operator.

"It certainly looks like it," the operator will reply. So far, so good.

The next man comes in and takes the elevator on its next trip. "What is it going to do—snow?" he will ask.

"It certainly looks like it," the man will reply. But he will tremble a bit.

The third member of the conspiracy will enter with "Well, what is this—spring?"

"I guess it is," the man will venture. "It certainly feels like it."

NUMBER FOUR: "Are we getting a little more winter for a change?"

OPERATOR *(quite nervous by now)*: "I guess we are. It certainly—" *(Trailing off into nothing.)*

NUMBER FIVE: "Going to have a little thunder-storm?"

OPERATOR: "I shouldn't be surprised—from the way it looks." (By this time the operator would be surprised at nothing.)

And so this would go on, until all possible combinations of contradictory weather predictions had been exhausted and the operator had stopped his car between the sixth and seventh floors on the way down and burst out crying, refusing to go down to the ground floor again. This ought to put a stop to all this nonsense.

So why don't about seven or eight of us give over a couple of months to this reform? We could all have lunch at some quiet place and then start out, in high good humor, to settle the weather problem once and for all, at least as far as elevator-men are concerned.

Garbled Favorites

A FEW nights ago I found myself, not very much to my surprise, singing in a loud voice from a pink song-sheet on which were printed the choruses to a batch of old-time favorites. There were lots of other people singing with me, so I could let go. I rather fancy myself at singing old-time favorites.

At least, I always had fancied myself, especially in the department of lyric-remembering. None of this "dum-de-dum-de-dum" for me. I sing the words right through from beginning to end, and have had many compliments on my memory. As yet no one has mentioned my voice, but I take that as a good sign.

However, on consulting the song-sheet (which I did more to humor the management than because I needed it) I was shocked to find that I have been singing the wrong words to many of my specialty numbers all these years. Not *all* wrong words, of course, but enough to make me stop and think.

I have, for example, been bellowing *In the Shade of the Old Apple Tree* with considerable confidence for over a quarter of a century, singing the ante-penulti-mate line so that it made no sense:

> *I could hear the dull buzz of the bee,*
> *In the blossoms that you sent to me*

whereas, of course, it should be sung:

8

I remember occasionally thinking that a bee in a nosegay was a bit out of place, but never stopped to consider also that, according to my version, the lady was sending the nosegay to the gent. In fact, the dangerous proximity of the bee had long ago ceased to worry me, and I have just been ploughing ahead, using my own version, and even teaching it to others. It rather frightens me when I think of it.

Singing old-time favorites

I have also been going hog-wild on *A Bird in a Gilded Cage*, singing "a pitiful sight" for "a beautiful sight," "she's not what she seems to be" for "she's not tho' she seems to be," and "she sold her soul for an old man's gold" for "her beauty was sold for an old man's gold."

In the last-mentioned mistake I have even been so

cocky as to laugh to myself at the ignorance of the writer in rhyming "soul" and "gold." You can't be much more unfair than to distort a lyric-writer's words and then blame him for not making them rhyme.

In *Break the News to Mother* I have been so wrong as to be incoherent. I have transposed lines, putting "just say there is no other" up in Line One, and, when I found myself stymied in Line Three, just repeating "break the news to mother" for good measure.

The first line to *Daisy* I have sung "Daisy, Daisy, give me your answer true" instead of "give me your answer, do." In *I Want a Girl* I have insisted on "a dear old-fashioned girl with eyes of blue" in place of the original "a good old-fashioned girl with heart so true." I have done those things which I ought not to have done and left undone those things which I ought to have done, and there is no health in me.

There is only one ray of hope for me in this song-sheet. According to it, the ante-penultimate line of *Yip-i-addy-i-ay* reads, "my heart wants to holler 'hurry'." Now, any printer who would set "hurry" for "hooray" is not infallible.

Possibly the whole song-sheet is wrong.

How I Create

IN AN article on How Authors Create, in which the writing methods of various masters of English prose like Conrad, Shaw, and Barrie are explained (with photographs of them in knickerbockers plaguing dogs and pushing against sun-dials), I discover that I have been doing the whole thing wrong all these years. The interviewer in this case hasn't got around to asking me yet—doubtless because I have been up in my room with the door shut and not answering the bell—but I am going to take a chance anyway and tell him how I do my creative work and just how much comes from inspiration and how much from hashish and other perfumes. I may even loosen up and tell him what my favorite hot-weather dishes are.

When I am writing a novel I must actually live the lives of my characters. If, for instance, my hero is a gambler on the French Riviera, I make myself pack up and go to Cannes or Nice, willy-nilly, and there throw myself into the gay life of the gambling set until I really feel that I *am* Paul De Lacroix, or Ed Whelan, or whatever my hero's name is. Of course this runs into money, and I am quite likely to have to change my ideas about my hero entirely and make him a bum on a tramp steamer working his way back to America, or a young college boy out of funds who lives by his wits until his friends at home send him a hundred and ten dollars.

106

One of my heroes (Dick Markwell in "Love's How-do-you-do"), after starting out as a man about town in New York who "never showed his liquor" and was "an apparently indestructible machine devoted to pleasure," had to be changed into a patient in the Trembly Ward of a local institution, whose old friends didn't recognize him and furthermore didn't want to.

But, as you doubtless remember, it was a corking yarn.

This actually living the lives of my characters takes up quite a lot of time and makes it a little difficult to write anything. It was not until I decided to tell stories about old men who just sit in their rooms and shell walnuts that I ever got around to doing any work. It doesn't make for very interesting novels, but at any rate the wordage is there and there is something to show the publishers for their advance royalties. (Publishers are crotchety that way. They want copy, copy, copy all the time, just because they happen to have advanced a measly three hundred dollars a couple of years before. You would think that printing words on paper was their business.)

And now you ask me how I do my work, how my inspiration comes? I will tell you, Little Father. Draw up your chair and let me put my feet on it. Ah, that's better! Now you may go out and play!

Very often I must wait weeks and weeks for what you call "inspiration." In the meantime I must sit with my quill pen poised in air over a sheet of foolscap, in case the divine spark should come like a lightning bolt and knock me off my chair on to my head. (This has happened more than once.) While I am waiting I mull over in my mind what I am going to do with my characters.

Shall I have Mildred marry Lester, or shall Lester marry Evelyn? ("Who is Evelyn?" I often say to myself, never having heard of her before.) Should the French proletariat win the Revolution, or should Louis XVI come back suddenly and establish a Coalition Cabinet? Can I afford to let Etta clean up those dishes in the sink and get them biscuits baked, or would it be better to keep her there for another year, standing first on one foot and then on the other?

You have no idea how many problems an author has to face during those feverish days when he is building a novel, and you have no idea how he solves them. Neither has he.

Sometimes, while in the throes of creative work, I get out of bed in the morning, look at my writing desk

108

piled high with old bills, odd gloves, and empty ginger-ale bottles, and go right back to bed again. The next thing I know it is night once more, and time for the Sand Man to come around. (We have a Sand Man who comes twice a day, which makes it very convenient. We give him five dollars at Christmas.)

Even if I do get up and put on a part of my clothes—I do all my work in a Hawaiian straw skirt and a bow tie of some neutral shade—I often can think of nothing to do but pile the books which are on one end of my desk very neatly on the other end and then kick them one by one off on to the floor with my free foot.

But all the while my brain is work, work, working, and my plot is taking shape. Sometimes it is the shape of a honeydew melon and sometimes a shape which I have never been quite able to figure out. It is a sort of amorphous thing with two heads but no face. When this shape presents itself, I get right back in bed again. I'm no fool.

I find that, while working, a pipe is a great source of inspiration. A pipe can be placed diagonally across the keys of a typewriter so that they will not function, or it can be made to give out such a cloud of smoke that I cannot see the paper. Then, there is the process of lighting it. I can make lighting a pipe a ritual which has not been equaled for elaborateness since the five-day festival to the God of the Harvest. (See my book on Rituals: the Man.)

In the first place, owing to twenty-six years of constant smoking without once calling in a plumber, the space left for tobacco in the bowl of my pipe is now the size of a medium body-pore. Once the match has been applied to the tobacco therein, the smoke is over. This necessitates refilling, relighting, and reknocking. The knocking out of a pipe can be made almost as important as the smoking of it, especially if there are nervous people in the room. A good, smart knock of a pipe against a tin wastebasket and you will have a neurasthenic out of his chair and into the window sash in no time.

The matches, too, have their place in the construction of modern literature. With a pipe like mine, the supply of burnt matches in one day could be floated down the St. Lawrence River with two men jumping them. . . .

When the novel is finished, it is shipped to the Cutting and Binding Room, where native girls roll it into large sheets and stamp on it with their bare feet. This accounts for the funny look of some of my novels. It is then taken back to the Drying Room, where it is rewritten by a boy whom I engage for the purpose, and sent to the publishers. It is then sent back to me.

And so you see now how we creative artists work. It really isn't like any other kind of work, for it must come from a great emotional upheaval in the soul of the writer himself; and if that emotional upheaval is not present, it must come from the works of any other writers which happen to be handy and easily imitated.

Toddling Along

WHAT is the disease which manifests itself in an inability to leave a party—any party at all—until it is all over and the lights are being put out? It must be some form of pernicious inertia.

Sometimes even my host asks me if I mind if he toddles along to bed

No matter where I am, if there are more than four people assembled in party formation, I must always be the last to leave. I may not be having a very good time; in fact, I may wish that I had never come at all.

But I can't seem to bring myself to say, "Well, I guess I'll be toddling along."

Other people are able to guess they'll be toddling along. One by one, and two by two, and sometimes in great groups, I watch them toddle along, until I am left, with possibly just my host to keep me company. Sometimes even my host asks me if I mind if *he* toddles along to bed. When this happens, I am pretty quick to take the hint.

I have often thought of hiring a little man to go about with me, just to say to my host: "Well, old Bob thinks he'll be toddling along now." It's that initial plunge that I can't seem to negotiate. It isn't that I *can't* toddle. It's that I can't *guess* I'll toddle.

*   *   *   *   *

I suppose that part of this mania for staying is due to a fear that, if I go, something good will happen and I'll miss it. Somebody might do card tricks, or shoot somebody else. But this doesn't account for it all. It is much deeper seated than that.

The obvious explanation to an analyst would be that I have an aversion to going *home,* because I have a sister fixation or am subconsciously in love with my parrot and am seeking an escape.

This, as I am so fond of saying to analysts, is not true. I would much rather be at home than at most parties. In fact, I don't go to many parties, and for that very reason.

My diagnosis would be that it is a sign of a general break-up. I have difficulty in starting to do anything, but once started, I can't stop. I find myself at a party and I have to stay at a party until I am put out.

The next step is, I am afraid, that I won't be able to find myself at all.

Oh, well.

Those Dicta

SCIENTISTS would get a lot farther with me if they didn't generalize so dogmatically. For every general dictum that they issue, at least three exceptions can be found right in my own house.

A Soviet psychologist has come out with one which sends me into paroxysms of rage every time I think about it.

"Brain sensitivity varies with the seasons," he says. "In the Spring the sensitivity of the brain is greatest, which explains why mankind always feels better in the Spring."

"Mankind," eh? Well, I, and at least eight other people that I happen to know, feel lousy in the Spring and top-hole in the Fall, and what do you know about that, you Communistic old doctor, you? Just because you happen to feel best in the Spring it turns out that "mankind" feels best in the Spring.

I don't know anything about my brain sensitivity (and, apparently, you don't either), but I do know that I reach my low point in May and am my peppiest in October. And I flatter myself that I am a member of that group which is known, euphemistically, as mankind. Not a member in very good standing, perhaps, but good enough to have a vote on the seasons. And I didn't give you my proxy, either.

Another dictum which makes me see red is the one

issued by all scientific analysts of humor, namely that the universal joke, the one thing that all "mankind" thinks is funny, is the sight of some one else slipping on a banana peel and falling. They always use this banana peel as the example, which is a tip-off in itself on their own range of humor.

I do know that I reach my low point in May

Now, I *don't* happen to think that it is funny to see anyone else slip on a banana peel and fall, and I know several other people who don't, either. I don't claim that we are right in this. All that I claim is that it is not the "universal joke." And I'll thank the learned humor-analysts not to go around saying that "everyone" laughs at it, and basing their theories on that premise.

115

"Mankind feels best in the Spring." "Everyone laughs at a man slipping on a banana peel." "All dreams are based on sex." "Self-preservation is the first law of mankind." With possibly fifty million exceptions.

The trouble with the specialists in what mankind does or does not do is that they don't get around enough with mankind.

My Face

MERELY as an observer of natural phenomena, I am fascinated by my own personal appearance. This does not mean that I am *pleased* with it, mind you, or that I can even tolerate it. I simply have a morbid interest in it.

Each day I look like someone, or some*thing*, different. I never know what it is going to be until I steal a look in the glass. (Oh, I don't suppose you really could call it stealing. It belongs to me, after all.)

One day I look like Wimpy, the hamburger fancier in the Popeye the Sailor saga. Another day it may be Wallace Beery. And a third day, if I have let my mustache get out of hand, it is Bairnsfather's Old Bill. And not until I peek do I know what the show is going to be.

Some mornings, if I look in the mirror soon enough after getting out of bed, there is no resemblance to any character at all, either in or out of fiction, and I turn quickly to look behind me, convinced that a stranger has spent the night with me and is peering over my shoulder in a sinister fashion, merely to frighten me. On such occasions, the shock of finding that I am actually possessor of the face in the mirror is sufficient to send me scurrying back to bed, completely unnerved.

All this is, of course, very depressing, and I often give off a low moan at the sight of the new day's metamorphosis, but I can't seem to resist the temptation to learn

One day I look like Wimpy

the worst. I even go out of my way to look at myself in store-window mirrors, just to see how long it will take me to recognize myself. If I happen to have on a new hat, or am walking with a limp, I sometimes pass right by my reflection without even nodding. Then I begin to think: "You must have given off *some* visual impression into that mirror. You're not a disembodied spirit yet—I hope."

And I go back and look again, and, sure enough, the strange-looking man I thought was walking just ahead of me in the reflection turns out to have been my own image all the time. It makes a fellow stop and think, I can tell you.

This almost masochistic craving to offend my own aesthetic sense by looking at myself and wincing also comes out when snapshots or class photographs are being passed around. The minute someone brings the envelope containing the week's grist of vacation prints from the drugstore developing plant, I can hardly wait to get my hands on them. I try to dissemble my eagerness to examine those in which I myself figure, but there is a greedy look in my eye which must give me away.

The snapshots in which I do not appear are so much dross in my eyes, but I pretend that I am equally interested in them all.

"This is very good of Joe," I say, with a hollow ring to my voice, sneaking a look at the next print to see if I am in it.

Ah! Here, at last, is one in which I show up nicely. By "nicely" I mean "clearly." Try as I will to pass it by casually, my eyes rivet themselves on that corner

9

of the group in which I am standing. And then, when the others have left the room, I surreptitiously go through the envelope again, just to gaze my fill on the slightly macabre sight of Myself as others see me.

In some pictures I look even worse than I had imagined. On what I call my "good days," I string along pretty close to form. But day in and day out, in mirror or in photograph, there is always that slight shock of surprise which, although unpleasant, lends a tang to the adventure of peeking. I never can quite make it seem possible that that is really Poor Little Me, the Little Me I know so well and yet who frightens me so when face to face.

My only hope is that, in this constant metamorphosis which seems to be going on, a winning number may come up sometime, if only for a day. Just what the final outcome will be, it is hard to predict. I may settle down to a constant, plodding replica of Man-Mountain Dean in my old age, or change my style completely and end up as a series of Bulgarian peasant types. I may just grow old along with Wimpy.

But whatever is in store for me, I shall watch the daily modulations with an impersonal fascination not unmixed with awe at Mother Nature's gift for caricature, and will take the bitter with the sweet and keep a stiff upper lip.

As a matter of fact, my upper lip is pretty fascinating by itself, in a bizarre sort of way.

The Soothsayer

IF BY any chance, you have any old diaries of yours lying around in a box, take my advice and don't start browsing through them. It is hard enough to keep one's chin up these days without digging back into the past to make a monkey of one's self.

I kept a diary from 1904 to 1921, more out of nervousness than anything else, and I give you my word a less important record has never been compiled. It would seem impossible to write over six thousand pages, covering some of the world's most momentous years, and still not have a single one worth reading, and yet I accomplished this herculean task. Even I was bored reading through them, so you can imagine how an outsider would take it.

On those pages where I was not being dull, I was being embarrassing. Almost any personal opinion set down in a diary reads like an extract from a high-school essay in ten years, but I outdid myself in immaturity. Aside from the language, which was of the early Penrod school, the opinions themselves were fatuous to the point of being almost pathological. I wasn't right once in seventeen years.

As no one else is ever going to get a look at these diaries so long as I have a bullet in my rifle, I will summarize for posterity my prognostications and meditations on world affairs, just to show how little a college education can do for a boy and, if possible, to keep future generations from committing themselves on paper. Following are some of the main points on which I allowed myself to give opinions:

As late as August 1st, 1914, I was adamant in my belief that there would be no war. My point (and I haven't the slightest inkling today of what went on in my mind when I made it) was that Wall Street would not permit it! Even without the written evidence of my diary, I went on record to this effect in a series of long talks given to my family during those nightmare days, in which scoffing at the very idea of war was the mildest of my methods.

Unfortunately I had to shout these opinions, as I was reassuring a deaf aunt, who had a daughter living in Paris at the time. "Don't you worry!" I yelled in her ear, in tones that rang up and down the coast of Maine. "There'll be no war!" And then I repeated my mysterious refrain, culled from some twisted corner of my brain: "Wall Street won't permit it!" As it turned out, I was wrong.

Once the war was on, however, I accepted my defeat good-naturedly and laughingly gave it six weeks. "Germany has put her foot in it," was my phrasing of the international situation, and, when England went in, I almost gave up reading papers, so sure was I that the thing was as good as over. I told my aunt this, too, and she stopped worrying.

We can pass over my tactical predictions in the conduct of the war with a lump generalization: "One hundred per cent wrong." America would not go into the thing. Wilson wouldn't permit it. (I had dropped Wall

Street by this time.) America would send an armada of airplanes in a non-stop flight across the Atlantic which would end the war in two days.

I was convinced that National Prohibition would never become a part of the Constitution (somebody, I've forgotten who, wouldn't permit it), and later I

"Don't you worry!" I yelled in her ear

gave it as my opinion that workers for Repeal were a lot of crack-brained visionaries.

"We in New York think that Prohibition is unpopular because we are in the center of anti-Prohibition sentiment. Wait until the Middle West is heard from! The Middle West will never permit Repeal! The Eighteenth Amendment may be modified but no one living today will ever see it out of the Constitution!"

Returning from Germany a few years ago last December, I smiled knowingly at the then current appre-

123

hension over Hitler's growing power. I happened to know, from private conversations with certain parties high in Berlin diplomatic circles, that the whole thing was a trick to let Hitler have a certain amount of power and then wait for him to hang himself with it. The hanging process would take just about six weeks, according to my reckoning.

With this record of prognostication behind me, I see no reason why I shouldn't team up with H. G. Wells on a book to be called "The World Tomorrow: A Glimpse into the Future." My luck has got to turn sometime. A man can't go on being wrong all his life. Or maybe I don't know my own strength.

What of Our Children?

IS LIFE made too easy for the youth of today? Are we raising a generation of pampered dawdlers? What is that on your necktie?

It seems to me that the harsh school in which I was brought up as a boy was the only one to train one for life in the raw. Nobody pampered me, I can tell you. I pampered myself.

I lived in a New England town which nestled among seven hills. It was often compared to Rome, Italy, by public speakers, because of the seven hills, but the life that we boys led was in no way comparable to the life led in the effete civilization of Rome. We derived from the more sturdy races of the Aegean, with quite an intermingling of Swedes and people from Providence, R. I.

The grammar school that I went to (Hard Knocks—1908) began at nine in the morning and was out at three in the afternoon. From then on we were forced to find something to do for ourselves. There was no catering to our tastes on the part of our elders as there is in the case of the children of today. We were on our own.

Mind you, there were no stream-lined roadsters then. No one owned a personal plane. No one had ever heard of a movie palace. The only movie that I ever saw as a boy was in the Eden Musee in New York, to which I was taken on vacations. It was a perfectly terrible movie, too. But all this deprivation gave me something, something that has stood me well in after life. It made a man of me.

When school was out we were forced to hitch rides on the backs of pungs if it was Winter, and on ice-wagons if it was Summer. This toughens a boy's stomach muscles and teaches him to like ice.

The more luxurious types of transportation not having been perfected we had to ride bicycles 'round and 'round, ringing the bells in unison. I have sometimes ridden a bicycle twenty-five times around a vacant lot, ringing the bell all the time. Hard though it was, I realize now that it steeled me for life's battle.

And look at what my hardy generation has done in its maturity!

It, together with the one just ahead of it, got us into a glorious war, raised the stock market to heights it had never dreamed of before, plunged us into the biggest depression the country ever had, and right now doesn't know whether it is afoot or good red herring.

Will the youth of today, with all its pampering, be able to carry on?

Why We Laugh— or Do We?

(Let's Get This Thing Settled, Mr. Eastman)

IN ORDER to laugh at something, it is necessary (1) to know *what* you are laughing at, (2) to know *why* you are laughing, (3) to ask some people why *they* think you are laughing, (4) to jot down a few notes, (5) to laugh. Even then, the thing may not be cleared up for days.

All laughter is merely a compensatory reflex to take the place of sneezing. What we really want to do is sneeze, but as that is not always possible, we laugh instead. Sometimes we underestimate our powers and laugh and sneeze at the same time. This raises hell all around.

The old phrase "That is nothing to sneeze at" proves my point. What is obviously meant is "That is nothing to *laugh* at." The wonder is that nobody ever thought of this explanation of laughter before, with the evidence staring him in the face like that.*

We sneeze because we are thwarted, discouraged, or devil-may-care. Failing a sneeze, we laugh, *faute de*

---

* Schwanzleben, in his work "Humor After Death," hits on this point indirectly when he says, "All laughter is a muscular rigidity spasmodically relieved by involuntary twitching. It can be induced by the application of electricity as well as by a so-called 'joke.'"

mieux. Analyze any funny story or comic situation at which we "laugh" and it will be seen that this theory is correct. Incidentally, by the time you have the "humor" analyzed, it will be found that the necessity for laughing has been relieved.

Let us take the well-known joke about the man who put the horse in the bathroom.* Here we have a perfect example of the thought-sneeze process, or, if you will, the sneeze-thought process. The man, obviously an introvert, was motivated by a will-to-dominate-the-bathroom, combined with a desire to be superior to the other boarders. The humor of the situation may *seem* to us to lie in the tag line "I want to be able to say, 'Yes, I know,' " but we laugh at the joke *subconsciously* long before this line comes in. In fact, what we are really laughing (or sneezing) at is the idea of someone's telling us a joke that we have heard before.

Let us suppose that the story was reversed, and that a *horse* had put a *man* into the bathroom. Then our laughter would have been induced by the idea of a landlady's asking a horse a question and the horse's answering—an entirely different form of joke.

The man would then have been left in the bathroom with nothing to do with the story. Likewise, if the man had put the *landlady* into the bathroom, the *horse*

* A man who lived in a boarding house brought a horse home with him one night, led it upstairs, and shut it in the bathroom. The landlady, aroused by the commotion, protested, pointed to the broken balustrade, the torn stair carpet, and the obvious maladjustment of the whole thing, and asked the man, confidentially, just why he had seen fit to shut a horse in the common bathroom. To which the man replied, "In the morning, the boarders, one by one, will go into the bathroom, and will come rushing out, exclaiming, 'There's a *horse* in the bathroom!' I want to be able to say, 'Yes, I know.' "

would obviously have been *hors de combat* (still another form of joke, playing on the similarity in sound between the word "horse" and the French word "*hors*," meaning "*out* of." Give up?).

Any joke, besides making us want to sneeze, must have five cardinal points, and we must check up on these first before giving in:

(1) The joke must be in a language we can understand.

(2) It must be spoken loudly enough for us to hear it, or printed clearly enough for us to read it.

(3) It must be about *something*. You can't just say, "Here's a good joke" and let it go at that. (You *can*, but don't wait for the laugh.)

(4) It must deal with either frustration or accomplishment, inferiority or superiority, sense or nonsense, pleasantness or unpleasantness, or, at any rate, with some emotion that can be analyzed, otherwise how do we know when to laugh?

(5) It must begin with the letter "W."*

Now, let us see just how our joke about the horse in the bathroom fulfills these specifications. Using the *Gestalt*, or Rotary-Frictional, method of taking the skin off a joke, we can best illustrate by making a diagram of it. We have seen that every joke must be in a language that we can understand and spoken (or written) so

* Gunfy, in his "Laughter Considered as a Joint Disease," holds that the letter "W" is not essential to the beginning of a joke, so long as it comes in somewhere before the joke is over. However, tests made on five hundred subjects in the Harvard School of Applied Laughter, using the Mergenthaler Laugh Detector, have shown that, unless a joke begins with the letter "W," the laughter is forced, almost unpleasant at times.

clearly that we can hear it (or see it). Otherwise we have this:

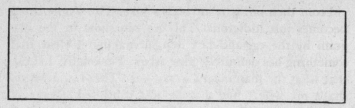

FIG. 1.

Joke which we cannot hear, see, or understand the words of.

You will see in Figure 2 that we go upstairs with the man and the horse as far as the bathroom. Here we become conscious that it is not a *true* story, something we may have suspected all along but didn't want to say anything about. This sudden revelation of *absurdity* (from the Latin *ab* and *surdus*, meaning "out of deafness") is represented in the diagram by an old-fashioned whirl.

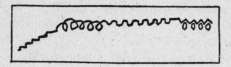

FIG. 2.

The horse-in-the-bathroom story under ideal conditions.

Following the shock of realization that the story is not real, we progress in the diagram to the point where the landlady protests. Here we come to an actual *fact*, or factual *act*. Any landlady in her right mind *would* protest against a horse's being shut in her bathroom. So we have, in the diagram, a return to normal ratiocination, or Crowther's Disease, represented by the wavy line. (Whoo-hoo!)

From then on, it is anybody's joke. The whole thing becomes just ludicrous. This we can show in the diagram by the egg-and-dart design, making it clear that something has definitely gone askew. Personally, I think that what the man *meant* to say was "That's no horse— that's my wife," but that he was inhibited. (Some of these jokes even *I* can't seem to get through my head.)*

* A. E. Bassinette, in his pamphlet "What Is Humor—a Joke?," claims to have discovered a small tropical fly which causes laughter. This fly, according to this authority, was carried from Central America back to Spain by Columbus's men, and spread from there to the rest of Europe, returning to America, on a visit, in 1667, on a man named George Altschuh.

Dress Complexes

THE theory that children's clothes may be responsible for some of their complexes in after life is the first sensible child-complex theory I have heard for a long time. I hate to think of what my Lord Fauntleroy suit did to me.

I had a suit which, from the pictures, seems to have been originally designed for Marie Antoinette's bedchamber. It had everything but the bed—and Marie Antoinette. It wasn't a suit. It was a production.

To make things worse, there was a rasher of curls that went with it. Now, my hair is not curly and never was. Through years of doing everything to it that scalp doctors tell one not to do I have managed to preserve it, but that is the best you can say for it. It is preserved. (*Pause for knocking wood.*)

The implication which suggests itself at my appearance in photographs of the period with long curls hanging down over my lace collar is too horrible to dwell on. It must have been deliberately —— I can't say it.

This get-up was, I hope, what was considered "formal dress," for I distinctly remember a blouse with a string around the bottom which was never quite strong enough to hold more than three dozen crab-apples, and I also remember the sound of corduroy pants rubbing together as I walked. This must have been my fatigue uni-

I have been known to sit for half an hour before a dress shirt

form. It also must have come later than the curls-and-canopy job.

Now, there were two complexes which this sartorial holdover from the Restoration might have left me. I think, at my age, that I may now safely say that it was the other one which fastened itself upon me. I get claustrophobia in a stiff shirt, and I do nothing about my cowlick.

I have been known to sit for half an hour before a dress-shirt fresh from the laundry, unable to bring myself to harness myself into it. If it has been so starched that the tops of the sleeves stick together, I *don't* get into it, although I have found that by dampening the offending portions with a sponge and crushing them in my hands the thing can be done as soon as they have dried. By then I am quite late to dinner.

Had it not been for that Fauntleroy suit with its Cluny collar and cuffs I might today be able to look as neat as the other boys. As it is, I shall have to go down in history as more the rugged type of dresser, asked only to clambakes and class smokers.

I might even be cited as "Mr. X." in a book of case histories dealing with complexes due to childhood dress. Still, I might have been in the other classification.

"East, West, Home's Best!"

IN CASE your house or apartment has begun to pall on you and you are getting sick of the same old molding and the same old windows every day, just notify an agent that he may bring people around to look the place over for rental. You'll want to stay then, just out of spite.

It's those glances that get your back up

People who are doing what is known as "looking at" an apartment are unpleasant people in the very nature of things. They are passing judgment on a place in which you have, for better or for worse, been living for some time. There's an insult, right there.

10

In the first place they always come "to look" when you are in your bare feet, or have half your face covered with lather. You may have thought that you kept the place fairly tidy, but the minute the "lookers" come in the door it takes on, even in your eyes, the appearance of a house in one of William Faulkner's novels, where poor mountain-white have been in-breeding and cooking pork chops for generations. You can tell that it wouldn't surprise them to see an old sheep stagger out of a corner.

    *   *   *   *   *

Then they begin. You try to pay no attention and to give them the run of the place by themselves, but you hear them whispering, or see them exchange glances. It's those glances that get your back up. Whatever you may pretend to be doing while they are looking (and it usually is something spurious, like winding your watch or patting down sofa cushions which don't need patting) you are burning up as you go through the motions.

"I suppose this is the dining room," the woman says. (She *supposes* it is the dining room! It's got a dining-room table and chairs and a sideboard in it, hasn't it? What does she want—a steaming roast ox spread out for her?)

"It's not very light, is it?" (It's light enough for *you*, old girl! You can stand a few shadows, with that pan!)

"It might be a little more cheerful with other curtains." (One of the reasons you want to leave may have been the dark dining room, but it now seems like a sun parlor to you. Other curtains, indeed!)

    *   *   *   *   *

Then they pass on into the kitchen, where they think they are out of earshot.

"Helma would never work here, I know." (And who is Helma to refuse to work in *your* kitchen? Better cooks than Helma have managed to whip themselves into working there.)

Then you hear an "Ugh!" No remark—just an "Ugh!" There certainly is nothing in that kitchen to go "Ugh!" about, unless she has got into the icebox

Then you hear an "ugh!"

and doesn't like cold beets. She'd better get out of that icebox or you'll have the police on her. She's not renting cold beets from you. She's not renting anything from you, if you have your way. You're going to stay right there yourself.

As they come back surprising you at your pillow patting you ask if they want to have you show them the

bedrooms. The woman smiles a nasty smile and says
no, they won't put you to that trouble, as they have
almost decided (*an exchange of glances*) that the place
is not quite large enough for them. They have a little
girl, you see. Well, it must be a pretty big little girl
to crowd them, in a place this size. Pretty big, and
pretty disagreeable.

* * * * *

So they leave, with polite thanks, which do not fool
you for a minute, and you come back into the dear
little nest that you call Home, and that you are going
to call Home for at least another year, God willing.

But you do take a little look into the kitchen to see
what that "Ugh!" was for.

How to
Understand Music

WITH people having the Very Best Music interpreted for them every Sunday afternoon over the radio by the Very Best Experts, it will soon be so that we can't hear "Turkey in the Straw" without reading a meaning into it. With so much attention being paid to *leit-motifs* and the inner significance of what the bassoons are saying, it would not be surprising if, after a while, we forgot to beat time. And if you don't beat time, where is your music?

I would like to take up this afternoon an analysis of Bach's ("Carry Me Bach to Old Virginny") symphonic tschaikovski in C minor, one of the loveliest, and, at the same time, one of the most difficult exercises for three-and-a-half fingers ever written. I may have to stop and lie down every few minutes during my interpretation, it is so exciting. You may do as you like while I am lying down.

In the first place, I must tell you that the modern works of Schönberg, although considerably incomprehensible to the normal ear (that is, an ear which adheres rather closely to the head and *looks* like an ear) are, in reality, quite significant to those who are on the inside. This includes Schönberg himself, his father, and a young man in whom he confides while dazed. What you think are random noises made by the musicians falling over forward on their instruments, are, when you understand them, really steps in a great, moving story— the Story of the Traveling Salesman who came to the Farmhouse. If you have heard it, try to stop me.

We first have the introduction by the woodwinds, in which you will detect the approach of summer, the bassoons indicating the bursting buds (summer and spring came together this year, almost before we were aware of it) and the brasses carrying the idea of winter disappearing, defeated and ashamed, around the corner. Summer approaches (in those sections where you hear the "tum-tiddy-ump-ump-tum-tiddy-ump-ump." Remember?) and then, taking one look around, decides that the whole thing is hardly worth while, and goes back into its hole—a new and not entirely satisfactory union of the groundhog tradition with that of the equinox. This, however, ends the first movement, much to the relief of every one.

You will have noticed that during this depicting of the solstice, the wind section has been forming dark colors right and left, all typical of Tschaikovski in his more wood-wind moods. These dark colors, such as purple, green, and sometimes W and Y, are very lovely once they are recognized. The difficulty comes in recognizing them, especially with beards on. The call of the clarinet, occurring at intervals during this first movement, is clearly the voice of summer, saying, "Co-boss! Co-boss! Co-boss!" to which the tympani reply, "Rumble-rumble-rumble!" And a very good reply it is, too.

The second movement begins with Strephon (the

eternal shepherd, and something of a bore) dancing up to the hut in which Phyllis is weaving honey, and, by means of a series of descendng six-four chords (as in Debussy's "Reflets dans l'eau" which, you will remember, also makes no sense), indicating that he is ready for a romp. Here we hear the dripping coolness of the mountain stream and the jump-jump-jump of the mountain goat, neither of which figures in the story. He is very eager (tar-ra-ty-tar-ra-ty-tar-ra-ty) and says that there is no sense in her being difficult about the thing, for he has everything arranged. At this the oboes go crazy.

I like to think that the two most obvious modulations, the dominant and the subdominant respectively, convey the idea that, whatever it is that Strephon is saying to Phyllis, nobody cares. This would make the whole thing much clearer. The transition from the dominant to the subdominant (or, if you prefer, you may stop over at Chicago for a day and see the bullfights) gives a feeling of adventure, a sort of Old Man River note, which, to me, is most exciting. But then, I am easily excited.

We now come to the third movement, if there is anybody left in the hall. The third movement is the most difficult to understand, as it involves a complete reversal of musical form in which the wood-winds play the brasses, the brasses play the tympani, and the tympani play "drop-the-handkerchief." This makes for confusion, as you may very well guess. But, as confusion is the idea, the composer is sitting pretty and the orchestra has had its exercise. The chief difficulty in this movement lies in keeping the A strings so tuned that they sound like B-flat strings. To this end, small boys are employed to keep turning the pegs down and the room is kept as damp as possible.

It is here that Arthur, a character who has, up until now, taken no part in the composition, appears and, just as at the rise of the sixth in Chopin's "Nocturne in E Flat" one feels a certain elation, tells Strephon that he has already made plans for Phyllis for that evening and will he please get the hell out of here. We feel, in the descent of the fourth, that Strephon is saying "So what?" Any movement in which occurs a rise to the major third suggests conflict (that is, a rise from the key-note to the major third. Get me right on that, please) and a similar rise to the minor third, or, if you happen to own a bit of U. S. Steel, a rise to 56, suggests a possibility of future comfort. All this, however, is beside the point. (Dorothy Angus, of 1455 Granger Drive, Salt Lake City, has just telephoned in to ask "what point?" Any point, Dorothy, any point. When you are older you will understand.)

This brings us to the fourth movement, which we will omit, owing to one of the oboists having clamped his teeth down so hard on his mouthpiece as to make further playing a mockery. I am very sorry about this, as the fourth movement has in it one of my favorite passages—that where Strephon unbuttons his coat.

From now on it is anybody's game. The A minor prelude, with its persistent chromatic descent, conflicts with the *andante sostenuto*, where the strings take the melody in bars 7 and 8, and the undeniably witty theme is carried on to its logical conclusion in bars 28 and 30, where the pay-off comes when the man tells his wife

142

that he was in the pantry all the time. I nearly die at this every time that I hear it. Unfortunately, I don't hear it often enough, or long enough at a time.

This, in a way, brings to a close our little analysis of whatever it was we were analyzing. If I have made music a little more difficult for you to like, if I have brought confusion into your ear and complication into your taste, I shall be happy in the thought. The next time you hear a symphony, I trust that you will stop all this silly sitting back and taking it for what it is worth to your ear-drums and to your emotions, and will put on your thinking caps and try to figure out just what the composer meant when he wrote it. Then perhaps you will write and tell the composer.

Truffle Poisoning

ONE of the easiest forms of pretense to break down is the pretense of enthusiasm for exotic foods. Just bring on the exotic foods.

When a man opens his eyes very wide and says, "Boy, what I couldn't do to a rasher of Japanese rollmops right now!" get him a rasher of Japanese rollmops and see what he does to them. The chances are that he can't gag down more than three mouthfuls.

Almost everyone has some little dish that he talks a lot about liking, because it is either hard to get or hard to swallow. But when they are confronted with their dream dish, it very often turns out that nausea flies in the window.

* * * * *

I used to rave a lot about truffles. (Incidentally, while raving, I mispronounced the word.) Now, all that I

I had to look as much like an ecstatic epicure as I could

144

actually knew about truffles was that they came as a fixing to several very tasty dishes. I had never really tasted a truffle on the hoof, but I had read about them, and talked as if all Paris knew of my craving for them.

Then, one night, I had my bluff called. A friend, with whom I was dining, said: "You ought to be very happy tonight. I see that they have truffles *au nature* on the menu." I said: "Oh, boy!"

There being very few things that I cannot eat with relish, I had every reason to believe that I could carry on with a truffle, even though I had never tasted one.

* * * * *

And I probably could have made a go of it if I had been in top form that night. But I was more in the mood to be pampered, and a plain truffle, although considered a delicacy, is not exactly succulent. It turned out to be something on the order of edible pumice, or a small, black sponge. It had no sauce. Just the pumice.

But I had to dig in and look as much like an ecstatic epicure as I could, smacking my lips and making French gestures with my free hand, while my companion watched with what I thought I detected to be high glee.

I was cured of my truffle talk, but I still have several dishes that I pretend to crave and which I hope I never have to eat under close scrutiny. One of them is *tête de veau*, or the head of a calf served with the brains, ears and eyes.

If you ever hear me raving about *tête de veau*, it will pay you to order me one and watch.

Word Torture

IN HIS column a short time ago Mr. O. O. McIntyre asked who could tell, without looking it up, the present tense of the verb of which "wrought" is the past participle. That was, let us say, of a Thursday. Today my last finger-nail went.

At first I thought that it was so easy that I passed it by. But, somewhere in the back of that shaggy-maned head of mine, a mischievous little voice said: "All right —what is it?"

"What is what?" I asked, stalling.

"You know very well what the question was. What is the present tense of the verb from which the word 'wrought' comes?"

I started out with a rush. "I *wright*," I fairly screamed. Then, a little lower: "I wrught." Then, very low: "I wrouft." Then silence.

From that day until now I have been muttering to myself: "I wright—I wraft—I wronjst. You wruft—he wragst—we wrinjsen." I'll be darned if I'll look it up, and it looks now as if I'll be incarcerated before I get it.

People hear me murmuring and ask me what I am saying.

"I wrujhst," is all that I can say in reply.

"I know," they say, "but what were you *saying* just now?"

"I wringst."

This gets me nowhere.

While I am working on it, however, and just before the boys come to get me to take me to the laughing academy, I will ask Mr. McIntyre if he can help me out on something that has almost the same possibilities for brain seepage. And no fair looking *this* up, either.

What is a man who lives in Flanders and speaks Flemish. A Flem? A Flan? A Floom? (This is a lot easier than "wrought," but it may take attention away from me while I am writhing on the floor.) And, when you think you have got it the easy way, remember there is another name for him, too, one that rhymes with "balloon." I finally looked that one up.

At present I'm working on "wrought."

Can We Believe Our Eyes?

I T IS pretty generally agreed by now that Seeing is not Believing. Along with those exploded saws (watch out for exploding saws!) that Old Friends Are Best and the Longest Way Round Is the Shortest Way Home (I could kill the guy who made that one up—it cost me eight dollars and a half in taxi fare once), the old dictum about seeing and believing has been shown to be just another flash in the pan.

In fact, according to scientists, if your eyes tell you that a thing is so, it is a very good reason for believing the opposite.

This will eventually make for a lot of trouble in the world.

However, all you have to do is to read the Sunday papers to see what little monkeys your eyes really are. Even the advertisements are getting into the game of confusing us with pictures showing large arrows and small arrows with captions like:

"Which is the larger of these two arrows?" Of course, it is perfectly obvious which is the larger, but when you come to measure them you find that, through some trickery, they are both the same size.

I will put up with just so much of this sort of thing, and then I will stop measuring.

This unreliability on the part of visual images is only

one part of Nature's way of making saps out of us, her children.

You may see two girls at a party, or two wire-haired fox terriers in a dog-shop window, and you say, pointing deliberately to one:

"The one on the right is the one for me. I can tell just by looking that this is what I have been searching for all my life." If you want to know what this leads to all you have to do is read the divorce notices or the list of wire-haired fox terriers for sale "cheap."

For example, take Figure 1 of the accompanying illustrations. Which of these acorns would you say was the taller? (One is a hydrant, but you are not supposed to know that.) You would naturally say that the acorn on the left was at least twice as tall as the one on the right. Taller and handsomer.

Well, you would be right. But, when you see two objects like these in an eye test, you *think*: "There is a trick here! I am supposed to say that the one on the left is taller, so it can't be. I will say the one on the right, much against my better judgment." And so you lose five dollars.

This is only one of the fascinating things that you can do with your eyes. Another is to wink one of them very slowly at a young lady sitting at the next table in a restaurant, and, the first thing you know, the other eye will be all blue and bulging and *very* sore, owing to her escort having shown you that optical illusion isn't everything. (See Figure 2.)

In Figure 3 we have another common form of self-deception. If you will take these concentric circles and rotate them slowly in front of your eyes, you will soon

149

be dizzy enough to be quite ill. (In order to rotate the circles it will be necessary for you to buy another copy of this book and cut out the diagram with a pair of scissors. If you try rotating the whole book, you will

FIG. 1

find, not only that you will get tired quickly, but that you will be unable to read the type matter. And as in the type matter are contained the directions for *stopping* the rotary movement, you may go on twirling the paper for hours without knowing what to do next.) But after you have rotated the concentric circles for some time, you will find yourself believing that the thing is *actually turning itself*! After a while you will think that you are

FIG.2

on a bicycle and will start working your feet on the pedals. If you keep the thing up much longer, you will faint.

Thus we see that our eyes play their pranks—as well as our other senses—and that the best thing to do with them is to keep them shut entirely.

150

There is a well-known case of optical illusion recorded in the files of the British War Office at the Old Vic. It seems that during the Crimean War a detachment of British troops was isolated in a lonely village in a clump of trees. (The natives were tree dwellers, silly as it may seem.)

They had nothing to do but drink a sort of mixture of heartsease (absinthe) and wormwood (absinthe) which the local doctor put up for people who had rather be dead.

Thus the days wore on.

One night when three subalterns were sitting around a fire and sipping at this strange mixture (no longer

FIG. 3

strange to them however, more like a mother), one, a sergeant (British spelling), Villiers, turned to his companions and said:

"Don't look now, boys, but there go the Devonshire Reds, all but O'Day."

(The Devonshire Reds was a regiment which was stationed in Ottawa at the time, and O'Day was the only man in the regiment whom Villiers knew.)

"I rather doubt if the Devonshire Reds are over here in the Crimea right at this minute," said Athoy, one of the three, "but I see what you mean. It is a body of moving figures going quickly, in a swaying motion, from left to right, but it is my guess that they are penguins.

"See! See! There is a penguin now—leading the band!"

The third member of the party, a Leftenant Merley, who had said nothing up until this time, still said nothing. It was later discovered that his mouth had, in some unaccountable way, sunk into his cartridge belt, making it impossible for him to talk. Furthermore, he didn't care.

But the two who had seen the passing regiment (of either Devonshire Reds or penguins) argued far into the night over the phantom marchers, and finally decided that they had been really nothing but a crowd of rather ungainly sheep, walking on their hind legs.

In the morning, however, it was found that, as far as the sentries knew, *nobody had passed through the camp at all!*

This, one of the most famous examples of optical illusion, is only one item in the testimony to back up the contention that we cannot believe our eyes. And if we cannot believe our eyes, what *can* we believe?

The whole thing becomes frightening once you start to think of it.

So don't think of it.

The Wreck of the Sunday Paper

WHAT is to be done with people who can't read a Sunday paper without messing it all up? I just throw this out as one of the problems with which we are faced if we are to keep our civilization from complete collapse.

There is a certain type of citizen (a great many times, I am sorry to have to say, one of the "fair" sex) whose lack of civic pride shows itself in divers forms, but it is in the devastation of a Sunday newspaper that it reaches its full bloom. Show me a Sunday paper which has been left in a condition fit only for kite flying, and I will show you an antisocial and dangerous character who has left it that way.

Such a person may not mean deliberately to do the things to a newspaper that he or (pardon my pointing) *she* does. They really couldn't achieve such colossal disarrangement by any planning or scheming. It has to come from some cataclysmic stroke of a giant force, probably beyond their control. Let them but touch a nice, neat Sunday edition as it lies folded so flat and cold on the doorstep, and immediately the rotogravure section becomes entwined with the sporting section and the editorial page leaps out and joins with the shipping news to form a tent under which a pretty good-sized child could crawl. The society page bundles itself up into a ball in the center of which, by some strange convulsion, the real-estate news conceals itself in a smaller and more compact ball. It is the Touch of Cain that these people have, and perhaps we should not blame them for it.

But they needn't *leave* this mound of rumpled newsprint this way. They could recognize their failing and at least try to correct its ravages before handing the paper on to someone else.

I once knew a man whose wife was a newspaper builder. She built things out of newspapers when she read them. There wasn't much to show for it when she had finished in the way of definite objects; that is, you couldn't quite make out just what she had thought she was building. But there had very evidently been some very clear idea of making each section of the newspaper into an object of some sort—anything so long as it made the newspaper absolutely unsuited for reading purposes.

Now the man usually tried to get down on Sunday morning ahead of his wife so that he could have first crack at the paper before the Great Disintegration set in. But, owing to a habit he had formed in his youth of staying out late on Saturday nights, he found it difficult to beat her to it. By the time he got downstairs the room looked like a militia encampment.

"What do you do with a newspaper?" he once asked her, as quietly as he could. "Try to dress yourself in it? You'll never get anywhere without buttons, you know."

But she didn't seem to mind his taunts, and, in fact, more or less put him on the defensive by calling him "an old maid"; so he decided that the time had come for action. He ordered *two* editions of each Sunday paper, one for his wife to mux about with and one for himself.

It was then that he discovered that his help-meet's rolling herself up in the paper was not just an unconscious weakness on her part but a vicious perversion from which she got a fiendish pleasure. She would sneak upstairs and get his personal edition before he was awake and give it the works, pretending that she couldn't find her own.

She was simply doing it to be mean, that was all. Often her own copy would be untouched and he would find it on Monday morning hidden away behind the sofa in its pristine smoothness.

I suppose, in a way, that the inability to read a newspaper which someone else has wrapped around himself or which is in any way disarranged is a sign of abnormality in itself and that we sensitive ones are in the wrong. All right, then—*I'm* the one to blame. *I'm* the enemy to society and the one to be locked up. But the fact remains that I am going to stand just so much more of this thing and then away *some*body goes to the police station.

Mistaken Notions

IF THERE is one thing that I resent (and there is), it is to be told that I resent being told anything. It drives me crazy.

I can take criticism and suggestions as well as anybody. In fact, the wonder is that I keep my head as well as I do, with all the criticism and suggestions that I get. But, frankly, I have just lost my temper and pretty badly, too. I have been told that I am "misinformed."

Somebody in a Sunday paper has got together a list of "mistaken notions," or things which ignorant people believe to be true, but which, according to this upstart, have no basis in fact at all. I find that I myself believe practically every one of them, which makes it more or less of an affair of honor between the author of the article and me.

* * * * *

His article is entitled, "How Badly Misinformed Are You About These Things?" The very tone of the title itself is offensive. "Misinformed," indeed! I think that I am the best judge of whether I am misinformed or not, and I'll take no back talk out of a Sunday feature writer.

The first point on which I am supposed to be "misinformed" is my belief that shaving makes hair grow faster. Well, Mr. Feature-writer, I happen to *know* that it does. He says that experiments have proved that it doesn't. And I ask you to read what his so-called "experiments" consist of:

"Any skeptic," he says, making a deliberate crack at me, "can test this easily by letting his whiskers grow for a year, cutting them off and weighing them, and then comparing this weight with the weight of bits of whisker shaved off every day for another year and carefully washed and saved."

In the first place, what does he mean by "easy" test? Washing, saving and weighing whiskers over a period of two years wouldn't leave much time for anything else, although a man who would set out to wash, save and weigh his whiskers would probably not have much of anything else to do with his time. Certainly nobody would employ such a man on any other kind of job. Nobody would want to have him even around the house.

In the second place, I happen to *know* that shaving does make hair grow faster, so Mr. Smart Alec can just wash, save and weigh his own whiskers and see if it makes any difference to me in my belief.

*   *   *   *   *

Another thing on which I am supposed to be "misinformed" is my belief that rainy weather is the cause of rheumatism and rheumatic pains. I don't know about its being the cause exactly, but I just wish that the author of that piece could have my knee on a good damp day. I wish that he could have it on *any* day, as a matter of fact, but I don't necessarily want to take his knee in exchange.

158

I'll bet he has an awful knee. I'll bet that he is a very disagreeable person to live with, constantly going about and saying: "You're misinformed—you're misinformed."

I am furthermore told not to believe that pin pricks with a brass pin are poisonous, that night air is injurious to sick people, that lightning never strikes twice in the same place, that dishonest people usually have a narrow space between their eyes and that fright to a mother before a baby is born is liable to mark the child in some way.

* * * * *

All right, I may believe these things and I may not, but from now on they are a part of my credo. I'll take no dictation from some whippersnapper on a newspaper. "Misinformed," am I? I'll misinform *him*.

The Calf in the Closet

FOR a man who is very fond of animals, I find myself oppressed by a strange phobia. I am afraid to go into my clothes-closet because there is a two-headed calf in there. Perhaps this needs a little explanation.

Several weeks ago I mentioned a birthday which was in the offing. It arrived, exactly on schedule, and with it several mementoes from loving friends, among them a two-headed calf. Perhaps this still needs a little explanation. I don't seem to be able to make it sound plausible.

On the morning of my birthday I was called on the telephone by a friend who asked me if I knew anything about getting people out of jail. The call was from the jail itself, and it transpired that two of my buddies were incarcerated there, and that I was indirectly the cause.

The day before, in passing a second-hand shop, they had seen a stuffed, two-headed calf among the chipped busts of Sir Walter Scott and suits of armor, and had decided that it was the very thing for a *cadeau* for old Bob on his birthday. The man in the store assured them that I was a very lucky fellow to be getting it, as he had had several calls to rent it out at three dollars a night. And, besides, it was a very attractive property in itself.

It being not a very large calf (about the size of a sheep-dog without foliage), they took it with them in their automobile, giving it a place of honor in the rumble seat. From then on their trail is a little obscured, but they took the gift about quite a bit, showing it off to various friends, doubtless amid good-natured laughter at my expense.

On their way home that night they found themselves (or rather, were found by a policeman) exceeding one of the more absurd speed limits in a suburban community, and were ordered to draw up to the curb. The officer, in that hail-fellow-well-met manner of traffic policemen, started searching the car for liquor.

He found no liquor, but he did find a two-headed calf, which confused him even more than a case of rye would have done. There being no specific charge of "driving an automobile with a two-headed calf," he arrested them on the more conventional charge of "drunken driving." When there is a two-headed calf in the rumble seat, it seems hardly necessary to look for liquor. They were not even given the benefit of a sobriety test. The cop was no fool.

So, on presenting myself at the station-house with my pockets full of gold pieces, I not only had the satisfaction of seeing my friends set free, but also of receiving the custody of the calf, with their blessings.

I took it with me into my automobile (that calf got a lot of riding, what with one thing and another) and took it home with me. Even then I wasn't really crazy about it, although I could see that it must have been cute when it was in the pink. But somehow a stuffed animal is not really the same sort of pal that a live one is.

Not having any precedent for bedding-down two-headed calves, I put my new-found treasure into my

161

clothes-closet—rather quickly, I am afraid. I turned its heads toward the wall, as there was a look about the four eyes that I did not like to think of as piercing the closet door in my direction when I was in bed. And then I shut the door and tried to forget.

But forgetting has not been easy. If I had left the thing out in the room where I could see it, I might have got up courage enough to take it out some day and

I circle even the vicinity of the closet

get that three dollars rental on it. But not being able to see it, yet knowing that it is in that closet, so quiet and static, with its tail turned toward me, has gradually got on my nerves. I have a feeling that it has turned around by now and is waiting, heads on, for me to open the door. And I cannot bring myself even to take a peek. A peek would be even worse than a bold sally into the closet.

I have now worn the same suit for nine days, and with the cool weather coming on, I am going to need a change pretty soon. But, with the passing of each day, the terror grows stronger, and I have now reached the point where I circle even the vicinity of the closet on my way in and out of the room. It is definitely beyond my powers to open that door, and what is more, I don't want to be anywhere near when someone else opens it.

I, who a short time ago, even doubted the existence of such a thing as a two-headed calf, am now reduced to a craven Frankenstein by the very proximity of one. (I didn't really create the monster—that took a trickier hand than mine—but I did bail it out of jail.)

So, anyone who feels the need of a stuffed two-headed calf may have one by calling at my room some day when I am out and opening the first closet door to the left. And even with the calf gone I shall never feel the same about that closet again.

How to Avoid Colds

THE prevalence of the common cold (or house-fly) at this time of year makes it advisable for everyone who possibly can to formulate a set of ten rules for their avoidance. At the end of the open season the best set of ten rules will be embroidered on a handkerchief and presented to their author to use for his own cold.

Here, as nearly as I can remember them, are my ten rules for avoiding the common head-cold:

1. Don't breathe through your mouth or your nose. These two orifices have been called "The Twin Roads to Germville" and, on a busy day, present a picture to the microscope similar to that of the Boston Turnpike. So long as people use their mouths and their noses to breathe through, we are going to have epidemics, plagues and eventual disintegration of the human race.

Your surgeon will be glad to fit you up with a small tube which can be inserted into the throat and worked with a nickel handpump. This will supply you with all the air you need for an ordinary day's breathing. Most of us get too much air anyway. Ordinary breathing air has been called "Nature's Exhaust," and the less we load ourselves up with the better.

2. Avoid crowds. This applies to all times of the year. You never know who may be in a crowd, and mingling with one may result in your being reminded of an old fifty-dollar loan or a promise to drop in and hear some-

one sing. Even if no one in the crowd has a cold, there is always someone who wants to push or romp, and you are pretty sure to have your hat knocked off. A good way to avoid crowds is to stay right in your room all day with the door locked.

3. Get plenty of sleep. When people come to awaken you in the morning, pull the covers up over your head and say: "Go away, I am avoiding a cold." When you have guests who hang around after midnight, excuse yourself politely by saying: "Now I will go in and get

Excuse yourself politely

my preventive sleep. This is the season for colds, you know." If, during the afternoon, you feel drowsy at your work, just put your head over on your desk and take a little nap. Your boss will understand if you put a little sign up by your elbow reading: "Men asleep here. Cold prevention."

4. Change heads frequently during the day. Have an extra supply of heads in your room (or in a large bag, if you travel about) and when you feel one stuffing-up, take it off and put on a fresh one.

5. Stay in a temperature of between 60 and 70 degrees. This can be done by jumping on board a train for Palm Beach and lying on the sand for a month or so. Be sure, however, to lie face up, with the arms outstretched, so that the sun can send its actinic rays across your chest and into your eyes. This is the hardest part of this rule to follow out. The temperature of the gambling rooms will be just about right in the evening, so you won't have to lie on your back there.

6. Don't dose up with patent medicines and nostrums. A sitz-bath of rock-and-rye twice a day, using ordinary care not to bruise yourself on the rock-candy, ought to be all the medicinal treatment you will need.

7. Eat a balanced diet. No proteins, no starches, no carbohydrates. Just a good steak with lyonnaise potatoes and asparagus now and then during the day. Remember the old adage: "Stuff a cold and stuff a fever."

8. No exercise. This is all-important. Exercise just stirs up the poisons in your system and makes you a hot-bed of disease. Sit, or lie, as still as possible, and smoke constantly. If you can stand it, have somebody read aloud to you. If you can't stand it, scream, "Stop that reading out loud!"

9. If you think that you have caught a cold, call in a good doctor. Call in three good doctors and play bridge.

10. And, above all, don't catch cold.

166

How to Kill Time

A TANTALIZING item appeared in the news columns a few weeks ago. It stated that an organization called the Leisure League of America had listed 700 ways of killing spare time, aside from plain frittering. Then it didn't say what they were.

It didn't even say what "plain frittering" was. How can you tell when you're frittering? A Senate Chamber full of busy statesmen can do a lot more frittering than a man with his feet on a rail and a straw in his mouth. I can fritter away an hour and then have to lie down and rest. Just because you're moving is no sign you aren't frittering.

But what about these 700 other ways to kill spare time? The Leisure League of America says it is going to get out pamphlets about them, but where are they? One of them is announced as "Hooked Rugs," which, I suppose, means that you can hook rugs in your spare time. Personally, I'd rather fritter than hook rugs, and I'm sure the rugs would rather I did, too.

In case I don't hear from the Leisure League of America before the end of the week, I am going to make up my own list of ways to kill spare time, because I can see a lot of spare time ahead of me and don't want to get caught short. It would be awful to have a lot of spare time on your hands and no way to kill it. Suppose you just *had* to hook a rug!

Here is a tentative list, which will need some going over and revision after I have talked to the authorities. There are certain additional things that I would like to do, but I am not quite sure what the city ordinances are on the subject.

1. Stringing wire paper-clips together to make a chain hundreds and hundreds of feet long. The longer the chain the less leisure time you have to kill.

2. Tooting an automobile horn in a stalled car.

3. Upsetting bookcases and then putting the books back in again, with each book opened at page 27.

4. Upsetting the bookcase again and putting the books back in, this time opened at page 45.

5. Running just as fast as you can to the end of the room and back.

6. Making tiny tinfoil balls (one-eighth of an inch in diameter) and snapping them at everyone you see who is over eighty. (You will have to make a lot of inquiries in this one, as a lot of people don't look their age.)

7. Rowing a rowboat without using the oarlocks.

8. Fishing without bait.

9. Walking up and down the aisles of a train, scanning each passenger's face and asking him, in a whisper, if he can tell you the lucky number.

10. Getting into an old sleigh stored in the top of a barn and singing "Jingle Bells!" and calling out "Giddyapp!"

11. Following fish up and down their tank in the aquarium and driving them crazy.

12. Breaking up saltine crackers.

Walking up and down the aisle of a train, scanning each passenger's face

13. Driving nails just as hard as you can into a board and then pulling them out.

14. Counting your fingers, omitting every second one.

By this time maybe the Leisure League of America will have issued its pamphlets and you can get down to work.

The Ten Most People

ON DISEMBARKING from the "Elsa Maxwell" yesterday, I was asked by a reporter to give my selections for a list of the ten most people in the world.

"The *ten* most?" I asked.

"Ten or eleven most," replied the reporter.

"I could name you the ten *least* people in the world," I said, throwing myself about the deck in a frenzy, "but the ten *most*—ah, that is a poser!"

"The word is *poseur*," said the reporter, batting an eyelash into left field.

"Let me see," I said, ignoring him and his monkey-shines, "I suppose that, at one point, Mrs. Dionne could have been said to be one of the ten most people in the world."

"I thought you'd pull a crack like that," he said, "and I came prepared . . . Smell this carnation!" And he held his lapel toward my nose.

I smelled the flower and a jet of black soot swept my features. I don't know what I was thinking of to fall for an old gag like that.

"That will teach you not to make cracks about the Dionnes in answer to a decent question," he said, as I relaxed.

"All right, seriously then," I said, although I felt anything but serious, "first among the most people in the world, I would nominate Amed Bey."

(I had him there, because I made the name **up out** of whole cloth, there being no such person as Amed Bey. The reporter, I knew, wouldn't want to confess his ignorance.)

"O. K.," he said, writing down the name Amed Bey. "Now we're getting somewhere! Who's next?"

I thought a minute. Then I rattled off, improvising as I went along: "Emil Grau, Paulette de Peu, Zemzi Janos, Leffington Mer, A. E. H. Tams, Mesmer Margmer, Mrs. Roger Freem, Roger Freem, Jr., and Manos Zofer."

"Good!" said the reporter, writing them down as fast as I made them up. "Now, you see what we can get done when you stop fooling?"

As he dashed off with his "scoop" for the "bulldog edition," I laughed quietly to myself, which was the only laugh of the afternoon.

Toning Down the News

THE publicity which American newspapers lavish on criminals is nothing compared to the indulgent tone taken by the French press toward the wayward boys and girls of Sunny France. Of course, it may be that, in reading the French papers, I do not always translate the words correctly, but, without looking them up in the dictionary, they seem to me to be extraordinarily mild words, considering the subject matter.

For example, *Le Courrier de Nice,* which is my favorite retailer of Gallic crimes, covers what are known as *crimes passionels* with great gusto and thoroughness under the general heading of *Faits Divers,* which seems to me to mean: "Various Goings-On" or "Odds and Ends of Action." This covers murder, arson, suicide and various forms of dismemberment—all, evidently, considered in the day's grist.

Under "Various Goings-On" we read the following headline (or *I* read it, anyway):

A SAD INDIVIDUAL IS ARRESTED AT MOUGINS

Putting two and two together, I made the story out to be, in part, as follows:

"Yesterday the police of Cannes had to occupy themselves with a sad individual (*triste individu*) living at

Mougins who was presenting himself with repugnant gestures," etc., etc.

As the story continues, we find that "repugnant gestures" is an understatement, even for the French Riviera, and that "sad individual" does not cover the case at all. It is quite possible that the individual may have been sad, or even moody, especially after the police occupied themselves with him, but gloominess did not seem to be his chief characteristic prior to his arrest.

Farther on, still under "Here and There in the News" we find a heading:

AN INDELICATE DOMESTIC AND HER SISTER ARE ARRESTED FOR THEFT

The "indelicacy" referred to consisted of stealing, over a period of three years, practically the entire movable equipment of the house in which one of them worked. Between them, the sad individual and the indelicate domestic could have played quite a good deal of havoc in a small town.

This genius for understatement continues in an account of a young man who found himself blown into two or three dozen pieces by an *engin explosif*, an accident, which moved the rewrite man of the *Courrier* to refer to him as "unlucky." Possibly a maniac who had butchered four or five people in a blind rage might be said to have "got out of the wrong side of the bed that morning."

Of course, there is always the chance that my knowledge of the French language does not do justice to the real meaning back of some of these mild terms for bold

174

actions, but it still would seem that the French press does not take violence and sudden death with quite the seriousness that it might. At least our newspapers call a spade a spade.

The Railroad Problem

I UNDERSTAND that there is a big plan on foot to consolidate the railways of this country into four large systems. This doesn't interest me much, as I walk almost everywhere I go. (I discovered that I was putting on quite a bit of weight and was told that walking was fine for that sort of thing, but, since making the resolution to walk everywhere I go, I find that I just don't *go* anywhere. As a result, I have gained six pounds and never felt better in my life.)

However, there must be people who use the railroads or they wouldn't keep blowing those whistles all the time. And it is in behalf of these people that I would like to make a few suggestions to the new consolidated systems, suggestions based on my experiences when I used to be a traveler myself. I jotted down notes of them at the time, but notes made on a moving train are not always very legible the next day, and I am afraid that I shall have to guess at most of them (especially those written with the pen in the club car) and rely on my memory for the rest.

What I want to know is—what are they going to do about the heating systems? In the new arrangement, something very drastic has got to be done about running those steam pipes under my individual berth. I have tried every berth from Lower One to Upper Fourteen on every line in the country except the Montour and the Detroit, Toledo, & Ironton, and in every damned one of them I was the central point for the heating system of the whole train.

It wouldn't be so bad if, when I had finally accommodated myself to lying beside a steam pipe by throwing off all the flannel pads which serve as blankets and going to sleep like Diana at the Bath (oh, well, not *exactly* like Diana but near enough for the purpose of *this* story), they didn't then run ammonia through that very pipe and set up a refrigerating system along about four in the morning. They might at least make up their minds as to whether they want to roast or freeze me. It's this constant vacillating that upsets me.

Now in this new system of railroads, while they are deciding so many questions, they might as well decide about me. I will be a good sport about it, whatever they say. But I *do* want to know what the plan is. Is it roast or freeze Benchley? Then I can make my own plans accordingly.

And while they are at it, they might work up some system of instruction which would eliminate new engineers taking their driving lessons on night runs. As I have figured it out, this is the way the thing is worked now:

The regular engineer takes the train until about three in the morning. Then the new man gets aboard and is shown the throttles and is instructed about how to put on his overalls and gloves. If the system is working well, this is the first time the new man has ever been near an engine in his life. A porter then comes rushing up from back in the train and announces: "O. K., boys! Benchley is asleep! Let-er ride!"

At this point the instructor tells the new man to start her up easy. The man, with that same enthusiasm which makes a beginner in automobile driving stall the engine right off the bat, starts "her" up as if he were trying to take off in a helicopter and rise right up off the ground. The result is that all the cars in the train follow for the distance of one foot and then crash together, forming one composite car.

"No, no, no, Joe!" shouts the instructor, laughing. "Take her easy! Let her in slowly. Look, let me show you!" So he does it, and the cars unscramble themselves and stand trembling, waiting for the next crash. I myself have, by this time, sat bolt upright in my berth in spite of a broken collar bone. It is not until I have snuggled down again that the novice up in the cab tries his hand again. This time he is a little better and gets the train ahead about ten feet before he forgets what to do next, grows panicky, and jams on his emergency. I venture to say that, on his second try, he sends me a good four inches into the headboard of the berth.

"At-a-boy, Joe!" encourages his mentor. "You'll learn in no time. Now, just give her one more bang and then I'll take it over. You've had enough for one night."

So Joe has one more, or maybe two more bangs

and then goes back to take his first lesson in coupling and uncoupling. This is no small job to undertake for the first time in the dark, and he does awfully well under the circumstances. All that he does is to drive the Anastasia into the Bellerophon so far that the occupant of Lower Two in the first-named car finds himself in bed with the occupant of Lower Fourteen in the second. Not bad for a starter, Joe. You'll be a brakeman *and* an engineer before you know it. (I take it for granted that it is the same pupil who is driving the engine and coupling the cars. There couldn't be *two* men like that on one train.)

Now, if there can be no way devised under the new system to have these new boys try out their lessons in some school in the yards, using dummy trains instead of real ones full of real passengers, then the least that the roads can do is to have the lesson hour come during the day when people are sitting upright and have a little resistance power. When these crashes come in the daytime (and they do, they do) you can at least brace yourself and look out of the window to see whether or not the train has landed in the branches of a tree. The new railroad systems should recognize that there is a time for work and a time for play and that four A. M. is *not* the time for romping among the younger engineers.

There are one or two other points which ought to be brought out in this little petition, points which the roads would do well to take to heart if steam travel is ever to supplant flying as a mode of transportation.

(1) Those two men who shout under my window whenever a train comes to a halt in a station during the night. I have heard what they have to say, and it really

179

isn't worth shouting. One of them is named Mac, in case the officials want to go into this thing any further.

(2) The piling up of bags in the vestibule by the porters on day trains. In the old days we used to carry our bags out ourselves, and, irksome as it was, we at least got out of the train. As it is today, the train has been in the station a good half hour before the porter has dug into the mountain of suitcases in the vestibule so that it is low enough for a man on a burro to climb over it. The roads should either add this half hour to

their running time on the time-tables (Ar. N. Y. 4:30. Disembark N. Y. 4:55) or else cut a hole in the roof to let out those passengers who have other connections to make.

(3) The polish used by porters in shining shoes. This

should either be made of *real* gum so that it will attract articles of value, like coins and buttons, or of real polish so that the shoes will shine. As it is, the shoes neither shine nor are they sticky enough to attract anything more tangible than dust and fluff.

Here again it is a case in which the roads must make up their mind. Before they can amalgamate they must make up their mind on a lot of things. I have already made up mine.

Route Nationale 14

How to Motor
from Cherbourg to Antibes via Cherbourg

COME with me and we will mótor through Sunny France, from the tippity-tip of Cherbourg to the top-*tip*pity-tip of Cap d'Antibes! Or come with me and we will go over to Dinty Moore's on Forty-sixth Street for some spareribs and sauerkraut. Anyway, we'll do *some*thing!

If it's motoring through France we're going, we shall have to get started earlier. We shall also have to have a motor. Perhaps we had better decide right now on Dinty Moore's.

To motor pleasantly from Cherbourg to Antibes, it is preferable to use one's own car, as in a rented French limousine the driver's mustache is always too big and too black. There really isn't much worry involved in taking your own car, unless you happen to be watching while they are lowering it down from the ship to the tender. Furthermore, in your own car, you don't care so much what the children do to the back seat

THE ARRIVAL

On arriving at the port of Cherbourg you are met on the tender by a representative of the A.A.A. who will tell you that your license-plates have just barely not arrived yet, but that they will be in tomorrow *très de bonne heure* (along about noon). So this means spending the first night of your motoring trip in Cherbourg (Grand Hotel du Casino, or behind the barrels on the new pier). Anywhere you stay, you get to know Cherbourg.

While roaming the streets of this quaint old seaport town (Napoleon said of it: *"J'avais résolu de rénouveller à Cherbourg les merveilles de l'Egypte,"* but he didn't quite make it, doubtless due to the lack of Egyptians), one can see much that is of interest—to the Cherbourgians. One may also *be* seen and pointed out as a native by the boat-train passengers as they roll slowly through the Main Street. ("Look, Harry," they say, "at those picturesque old natives! Don't those people *ever* bathe, do you suppose?") One can also get a line on the boat-train passengers themselves from the outside. They don't shape up so hot, either. (Beauty note: Every woman looking out at the windows of the incoming boat-train has just been freshly lip-sticked in preparation for embarkation.)

A good place to spend the evening while waiting in Cherbourg is not the Café de Paris across the bridge. It isn't much fun in the Grand Hotel du Casino, either. But you are all excitement at the prospect of your early start in the morning, so it's early to bed, after a chat with the quaint old negro concierge from Philadelphia, Pa.

At seven o'clock you are up and ready, with everything strapped on the car and the children buried in the back seat under the extra hampers and coats. (One child is buried so deeply that he is a great big boy by the time he is remembered and dug out.) The maps are spread open and a schedule arranged which calls for lunch at Lisieux. (Hotel France et Espagne. Bad Martinis.) A light rain is falling.

At the *mairie* it will be found that the license-plates have not yet come, and eighteen shoulders will be shrugged. The car will then be driven back to the hotel (Grand Hotel du Casino, 100 fr.) and a more thorough tour made of

CHERBOURG (¼ kms.). A quaint seaport town, of which Napoleon once said: "*J'avais résolu de rénouveller à Cherbourg les merveilles de l'Egypte.*" It was his intention to revive in Cherbourg the marvels of Egypt is the way it looks. You may see a statue of Napoleon in the public square across the bridge. On the other hand, you may not. You may also see Pauline Frederick in "The Woman Thou Gavest Me," the film for which was found in an old bureau drawer by the exhibitor. Then there is always the Café de Paris. And the Grand Hotel du Casino.

The license-plates not having come at fifteen o'clock, it is decided to spend the night in

CHERBOURG (¼ kms.). A quaint seaport town which Napoleon once designated as the place where he was to revive the marvels of Egypt. To this end he appointed Vauban, the great engineer, to construct fortifications and plan a harbor which should be impregnable. (You learn a little more each day you stay in Cherbourg. By the time I left I was being groomed as Opposition candidate for Mayor. I was letter-perfect in the opposition, but my age was against me.)

During the second evening in Cherbourg, after seeing

that everything is going all right at the Café de Paris, you can read up on the rules of the road, some of the most readable being:

1. In France one keeps to the right, except when skidding.

2. Danger signals along the road are represented by black triangles with little pictures on them. Be careful not to become so interested in looking at the pictures that you forget the danger. A picture of two little hills side by side (these French!) means *cassis*, or a gully across the road (Cassis, in vermouth form, also makes a nice gully across the road if taken in sufficient quantities). A cute little gate means a *passage à niveau gardé* or protected level crossing. An even cuter choo-choo (if you are traveling with children), with smoke and everything, means an unprotected level crossing. This is the one you mustn't get too fascinated by.

3. The way to say "dust clip of front hub" is *"ressort cache poussière de moyeu avant,"* something you really don't have to learn as you can always point. In case you end up in Holland the way to say it is *"Sluitveerje der smeeropening,"* which is just plain silly.

4. Gasoline is sold by the *bidon*. Be careful about this.

5. An automobile tourist arriving in France on March first for a four months' visit will take out a *laissez-passer* for thirty days. This immediately puts the tourist under suspicion in the eyes of all officials and sometimes ends in his incarceration.

By this time it is bedtime, as you have to make an early start in the morning. There are very tall hat-racks in each bedroom of the Grand Hotel du Casino, from which you may hang yourself if you have to stay a third day in Cherbourg.

Up at seven, in a light rain. A chat with the colored concierge from Philadelphia, one last look around at the Café de Paris, a visit to Napoleon's monument to make sure what it was he hoped to make out of Cherbourg, and, at eleven o'clock sharp a trip to the *mairie* where there is tremendous excitement owing to the arrival of the license-plates. By this time you have made such friends with every one in the place, including the Mayor, that it costs you three hundred francs in tips. The adjusting of the plates, the signing of the Peace Treaty, the shaking hands and the shaking-down, take an hour and a half, so it is decided to have lunch at the

GRAND HOTEL DU CASINO (35 fr.). A quaint old hostelry situated hard by the *quai* overlooking the harbor fortifications built for Napoleon by Vauban, the great engineer.

THE START

Leaving Cherbourg, believe it or not, we ascend a gentle grade along winding roads through picturesque Normandy (light rain). The excitement of actually riding in a moving automobile proves too much for the children and a stop has to be made just this side of

BAYEUX, famous for its tapestry and cathedral, neither of which we see. The excitement of passing through a French town other than Cherbourg is too much for the children and another stop has to be made just the other side of

BAYEUX, famous for its tapestry and cathedral, although there was a perfectly good hotel (Hotel de

Luxembourg) on the way through. At this point it is discovered that the "funnies," bought in an American newspaper the day before in Cherbourg, have been packed in a suitcase on the trunk rack, necessitating taking the car apart to get them. From here on the children are engrossed in reading American "funnies," which gives us quite a stretch without a stop to

CAEN (pronounced "Kong"), famous as being the first train-stop from Cherbourg to Paris, where most American tourists think they are in Cayenne.

Engrossed in reading American "funnies"

Stop for the night at LISIEUX (scheduled for lunch the day before). Hotel France et Espagne. (Bad Martinis.) The residents of Lisieux sleep all day in order to be abroad all night under the windows of the Hotel France et Espagne (under the window of Room 34 in particular), where they walk up and down in an especially whittled type of sabot, pinching children to make them cry. Some also carry small horns or attach even smaller ones to bicycles, thereby effecting a squeak in synchronization with the bicycle wheels. This causes the fox terrers (an exceptionally repulsive breed, fat and soiled) to bark, which, in turn, causes the children to cry.

Up at four (bad Martinis) and on the road at five-thirty, passing through such interesting towns as Ĕvreux, Mantes, Flins, and St. Germain-en-Laye, none of which are seen owing to the entire family catching up on last night's sleep.

We are awakened by the sound of heavy traffic and, on inquiring where we are, are told that we are in Paris (Porte Maillot).

Here ends the first stage of our automobile tour from Cherbourg to Antibes. The stay in Paris is regulated by the length of time it takes to recover the use of our limbs and have the *ressort cache poussière de moyeu avant* fixed. The number of remaining checks in the A. B. A. book has also something to do with it.

Continuation of Tour
(Paris to Antibes)

The P.L.M. train (*Wagon Lits*) leaves Paris (Gare de Lyons) at 19:40, arriving at Cannes at 11:02 the next day. Fifteen minutes motor trip to Cap d'Antibes.

Little Noise Abatement

SO NOW we are to have no more noise. Scientific research has disclosed the fact that the effect of harsh noises on the brain is more deleterious than that of drugs, and nowhere near so pleasant while it is happening. The bursting of a paper bag, according to the Noise Abatement Commission, increases the brain pressure more than does morphine, but you don't read of anyone smuggling paper bags into the country just to bang them in some addict's ear at so much per bang. Noise is bad for you and isn't even any fun. It's a wonder that they care about prohibiting it.

Doing away with banging paper bags is a good beginning, along with sidewalk loudspeakers and other public disturbers, but why not first do away with the people who think it is funny to bang paper bags? You would find that you were killing about 500 birds with one stone, for they are the ones who make almost all other kinds of obnoxious noises. Anyone who thinks it is funny to sneak up behind you and whack an inflated paper bag (and is there anything more satisfactory than to see the chagrin on his face when the bag turns out to be a dud and refuses to bang?) will also sneak up behind you and push you off rafts into the water, will dive down and grab your legs while you are swimming, will snap rubber bands at you, and will cover his lower teeth with his lip and emit piercing whistles. Get rid of one and you will have got rid of them all.

This shrill whistling through the teeth is a sure indication in a boy that he will grow up to be an obnoxious citizen. They usually practice it in public gatherings where it will attract attention to themselves. It is offered in place of any mental attainment or physical prowess and is almost always the mark of retarded development along lines other than whistling through the teeth. In a crowd, if you will watch carefully, you will see the boy who has just whistled himself into prominence sooner or later will begin to push. This is also considered funny, especially if a good flying wedge can be started which will knock over a couple of old ladies. It is all a part of the banging-paper-bags and whistling-through-the-teeth psychology and is, mental experts will tell you, the sign of an inferiority complex. Inferiority is a mild word for it.

What the scientists do not seem to have taken into consideration in their researches is that it is not so much the noise itself that irritates as the knowledge that someone is making the noise deliberately.

That it is entirely a question of whether the noise is necessary or not is shown by the fact that I am not upset by the sound of celery or nuts being eaten. There is no way that I know of, unless they are ground up into a paste and dissolved in the mouth, by which celery and nuts can be eaten noiselessly. So my nerves get a rest during this course, and I have nothing but the kindliest feelings toward the eater. In fact, I don't hear it at all. But ice-crunching and loud gum-chewing, together with drumming on tables and whistling the

190

same tune seventy times in succession, because they indicate an indifference on the part of the perpetrator to the rest of the world in general, are not only registered on the delicate surface of the brain but eat little holes in it until it finally collapses or blows up. I didn't see this mentioned anywhere in the Commission's report.

The Commission, in fact, just concentrates on the big noises, like those which go to make up what poets call "the symphony of a big city." Some of these are also the result of the activities of grown-ups who used to whistle through their teeth when they were boys and who now don't care how much they disturb other people so long as they call attention to themselves. In this class are those owners of radio supply shops who stick big horns out over their doors to give "Anchors Aweigh" an airing from nine to six every day; chauffeurs who sound their horns in a traffic jam when they know that it will do no good; and, I am sorry to say, mendicants who walk up and down the street playing shrill little instruments featuring The Blue Danube Waltz and Happy Days in rotation.

I hate to be nasty about blind men (if they really are blind) but there is one who takes up a stand right under my window on Tuesdays, Thursdays, and Saturdays and plays a clarinet most of the afternoon. He is accompanied by a helper with a banjo.

Now, a clarinet is an instrument with considerable volume and powerful reach. It sounds out above the noise of the elevated (which I don't mind) and the riveting (which I can make allowances for) and the worst of it is he plays it pretty well. When it first begins

I rather enjoy it. I stop my lathe and hum softly to myself. I sometimes even get up and execute a short *pas seul* if nobody is looking. But his repertory is limited, and, after a while, I'm Dancing with Tears in My Eyes Because the Girl in My Arms Isn't You loses its sentimental value and begins its work on my nerve fibers. I try to say to myself: "Come, come, the man is blind and very poor," but then I remember reading about street beggars who not only are really not blind but who make more in a day than I do in some weeks (this week, for instance) and I become convinced that this man is one of those. And why can't he move on? Doesn't he ever stop to think that there are probably 5,000 people who are being driven mad by his music within a radius of one block? Aren't there *any* instruments that he can play which aren't so loud? By this time I am in a rage which is cumulative every time he stops and I hear him begin again. (The stopping and beginning again is really the peak of the irritation.) The whole thing ends in my shutting all the windows and getting under the bed to sulk.

I hope that the Noise Abatement Commission will take cognizance of these things. If they don't, I have my own resources. I have a small rifle with which I am practicing every day at the shooting gallery, and I am going to try it out on that newsboy (aged thirty-five, with a voice to match) who picks out the noon hour about once a week to walk through my street announcing that "Nya-a-ya-nyaded! Onoy-nad-ed!" in tones which would indicate that he has three other men inside him. I may not wait for the Noise Abatement Commission to get him.

As a matter of fact, I have every confidence that some of the louder and more general noises will be abated. It is the little noises that I am after, or rather the people who make the little noises. My brain cells are pretty far gone as it is, but it may not be too late. Of course, the question might arise as to what I shall use my brain for, once I have saved it. There will be time enough to figure that out when the noises have stopped.

Culture

SOMEBODY has sent me (doubtless with a good idea in mind) a folder called "Are You at Ease with Cultured People?" Without looking inside I can answer "No."

Then follows a list of subjects which are supposed to constitute the conversational material upon which "social gatherings" are based. It is asked "What Do You Know About——"

(1) The Nine Greek Muses. I didn't even know they were sick.

(2) The poetess called "The Tenth Muse." O. K. What?

(3) The SPECIAL SIGNIFICANCE of *The Golden Ass*, by Lucius Apuleius. (You can get some idea of the people who made up this list by the fact that "special significance" is capitalized. George Ade must have had a hand in it).

(4) Boreas, Charon, Cytherea, Dryades, Galatea, Pandora, Parnassus, Styx, Thisbe. If knowing about these constitutes culture, then my small son is the most cultured man in Westchester county.

(5) Machiavelli, *Poema del Cid, Sturm und Drang,* Troubadours, Pascal, George Sand, Proust, *The Dunciad, Tale of a Tub*. All drunkards.

(6) THE WAY a sonnet rhymes. A-B-A-B-A-A-B-B-B-A-W.

194

"Are you at ease with cultured people!"

(7) Dionysian revels. Is that a nice question?

(8) Mary Pickford's real name. Now you're talking. Smith.

(9) The various schools of the modern theatre. The Sargent School, Ned Wayburn's Tap Dancing School, the Hasty Pudding and the Mask and Wig.

(10) The greatest opera writer. Probably the most ignorant question ever asked.

(11) Font, a pica, an em. Well this is set in 11 point Baskerville, and if you don't know about a pica and an em you don't do any crossword puzzles.

(12) The discovery of the telescope. Well, an old fellow was fooling around one day with a mirror and he happened to look into it upside down. "What's all this?" he said, "I'll bet I could work up a telescope out of what we've got here." "Work up what?" asked his wife. "A telescope," said the old chap. "You go upstairs and lie down," said his wife. So he did, and when he came downstairs again he had a telescope. (Sorry you asked?)

There are a lot of other questions listed, but you wouldn't be interested any more than I was. A footnote says that "these topics, chosen at random, are constantly mentioned in cultivated society." Can you imagine a worse party than one at which they were being constantly mentioned?

I once went to a party at which cultivated people were as thick as fleas. The whole evening was spent in trying to use the word "honkey-tonk" in a sentence. When I got home I called up a few cronies and we had a good long talk about the Nine Greek Muses.

The Real Public Enemies

I HAVE now reached an age when I feel that I am pretty well able to take care of myself against animate enemies. By "animate enemies" I mean living people, like burglars, drunks, or police—people who set out with a definite idea in their minds of getting me. Mind you, I don't mean that I can lick these people in a hand-to-hand encounter, but I do know, in a general way, what to do when they attack me, even if it is only to run.

It is the inanimate enemies who have me baffled. The hundred and one little bits of wood and metal that go to make up the impedimenta of our daily life—the shoes and pins, the picture books and door keys, the bits of fluff and sheets of newspaper—each and every one with just as much vicious ill will toward me personally as the meanest footpad who roams the streets, each and every one bent on my humiliation and working together, as on one great team, to bedevil and confuse me and to get me into a neurasthenics' home before I am sixty. I can't fight these boys. They've got me licked.

When I was very young and first realized the conspiracy against me on the part of these inanimate things, I had a boyish idea that force was the thing to use. When a shoestring had clearly shown that it was definitely *not* going to be put through the eyelet, I would give it a yank that broke it in two, and feel that the bother of getting a new lace was not too much to pay for the physical pain which the old lace must have suffered. In fact, as I put in the new one I had an idea that it was pretty well frightened at the example of its predecessor and would jolly well behave itself or suffer the same fate.

But after years of getting out new laces and buying new fountain pens (my method, when a pen refused to work, was to press down on it so hard that the points spread open like a fork and then to rip the paper in a frenzied imitation of writing), I gradually realized that I was being the sucker in the battle and that the use of force didn't pay in the long run.

I then started trying subtlety. If there is one field in fighting in which a human ought to be able to win out over a piece of wood, it is in tricky maneuvering. Take, for example, when you are trying to read a newspaper on top of a bus. We will start with the premise that the newspaper knows what you are trying to do and has already made up its mind that you are not going to do it. Very well, Mr. Newspaper, we'll see! (Later on you don't call it "Mr. Newspaper." You call it "you —— —— —— ——!" But that is after you know it better.)

Suppose you want to open it to page four. The thing to do is not to hold it up and try to turn it as you would an ordinary newspaper. If you do, it will turn into a full-rigged brigantine, each sheet forming a sail, and will crash head-on into your face, blinding you and sometimes carrying you right off the bus.

The best way is to say, as if talking to yourself, "Well, I guess I'll turn to page seven." Or better yet, let the paper overhear you say, "Oh, well, I guess I won't read any more," and make a move as if to put it away in your pocket. Then, quick as a wink, give it a quick turn inside out before it realizes what is happening.

It won't take it long to catch on, but, thinking that you want to turn to page seven, as you said, it will quite possibly open to page four, which was the one you wanted.

But even this system of *sotto voce* talking and deceit does not always work. In the first place, you have to have a pretty young newspaper, who hasn't had much experience, for all the older ones will be on to your game and will play it back at you for all it is worth.

The only way to be safe about the thing is to take it all very calmly and try to do your best with deliberate fierceness, folding each page over under your feet very slowly until you come to the right one. But by that time you have got the paper in such a condition that it cannot be read—so you lose anyway.

Of course, after years of antagonizing members of the inanimate underworld, you are going to get an active conspiracy against you, with physical violence on *their* part as its aim. It then becomes, not an aggressive campaign on your part, but one of defense to save yourself from being attacked.

For example, I have a pair of military brushes which have definitely signed up to put me on the spot and will, I am afraid, ultimately kill me. I have taken those brushes from the bureau and held them in a position to brush my hair, without an unkind thought in my mind, and have had them actually fly out of my hands, execute a pretty take-off of perhaps a foot and a half, and then crash into my forehead with as deft a "one-two" as any heavyweight ever pulled on a groggy opponent.

I have placed slippers very carefully under my bed, only to have them crawl out during the night to a position where I will step into them the wrong way round when leaping out of bed to answer the telephone.

These things don't just happen, you know. They are proofs of a very clear conspiracy to hurt me physically which exists among household objects, and against which I have no defense. All that I can do is to walk about all day crouched over with one elbow raised to ward off the heavier attacks which are being aimed at me. This gives a man a cringing look which soon becomes a personal characteristic.

It is this element of physical danger which has entered my struggle with these things which has got me worried.

I will match myself in an unequal fight to open a can of sardines or a bottle of water, if the issue is to be merely whether I get it open or not. But I can't face the inevitable gashing and bleeding which always follow my failure. I will tackle the closing of a trunk or suitcase, but I am already licked by the knowledge that, no matter how the fight turns out, the metal snaps are going to reach out and nip my fingers.

The only thing that I can do, as old age and experience bear down on me, is to sit with my hands in my pockets and try nothing.

I have said that, in my youth, I gave up the use of force when little things thwarted me. I *should* have given it up, but there is one enemy which I still lash out at in futile bludgeonings. It is the typewriter on which I am writing this article. In putting on a ribbon

I lose myself entirely, and invariably end up completely festooned like Laocoön, ripping and tearing madly with ink-stained fingers at a ribbon which long before I had rendered useless. I am also thrown into raging fits of physical violence when, owing to some technical fault which I do not understand, the letters begin getting dimmer and dimmer, finally becoming just shells of their natural selves. On such occasions I start very quietly hitting the keys harder and harder, muttering, "Oh, you won't, won't you?" until I am crashing down with both fists on the keyboard and screaming, "Take that—and *that*!"

In fact, as I write this, I detect a weakening in the pigment of the ribbon, and, as I strike each key, less and less seems to be happening. I will try to be calm.

I must try to remember that it does no good to inflict pain on inanimate things and that the best that I can do is break the typewriter . . . But really . . . after all . . . you xxxxx you xxxxxxxxxxxx take that xxxxxxxxxxxx and *that* xxxxxxxxxxxx.

Love in Hollywood

THE seeming prevalence of divorce in Hollywood may be explained away by the fact that Hollywood divorces rate more publicity than any others, and so just seem more prevalent. But this does not explain why people in the movie colony can't get engaged, married or divorced without putting on a routine. You would think that they were smuggling opium into the country, the way they duck back and forth.

Nobody in Hollywood ever just goes and gets married, the way people do in other parts of the country. They never even get engaged. It takes at least six months for the male to circle around the female and dart away again, like polyps or Japanese sand-fish. It must be the climate.

Let us say that Norman LeRoy and Maida Marston work together in a picture and, what with the heat of the lights and the necessity for re-takes, find that they are in love with each other. There certainly is no harm in that. Well, there is harm in it, but it's done all over the world, and with much more directness. Joe Doaks and Meridian Blevitch, of Utica, N. Y., fall in love, too.

As is customary under such circumstances, Norman LeRoy and Maida Marston see a lot of each other at the Cocoanut Grove and other public places; for, after all, that's the whole idea of liking someone, isn't it? They are seen dancing together, eating together and, if you happen out on the porch suddenly, necking together. This, my spies tell me, is only what goes on everywhere.

But, when confronted with the evidence, Miss Marston says: "I like Norman very much, but we are just good friends." And Norman says: "I never heard of Miss Marston, except professionally." This goes on for a few weeks, and they become engaged to be married.

Now, becoming engaged to be married has, with the

"Miss Marston? Never heard of her—except, of course, professionally"

broadening of our standards, been accepted as quite *au fait*. It is even the conventional thing to do. But Mr. LeRoy and Miss Marston shun the reputation for it as they would the reputation of being lepers. When discovered at Palm Beach together, Miss Marston says: "Of course, I am very fond of Mr. LeRoy, but we are

204

just good friends." And Mr. LeRoy says: "Who? Miss Marston? Never heard of her—except, of course, professionally."

Eventually, as so often happens in cases of engagement, they get married. A mistake, perhaps, but who can cast even the second stone? So, when they are man and wife, Mr. LeRoy takes up his legal residence at the Hollywood Athletic Club and Miss Marston goes to her mother's. And, when confronted with the city clerk's ledger and the minister's day-book, Mr. LeRoy says: "I am flying today to New York, where I am taking up sword-fishing. I have only the best wishes for Miss Marston, of whom I have never heard." And Miss Marston says: "Business calls me today to New Rochelle, N. Y. I am flying, but I had no idea that Mr. LeRoy was going to be on the same plane. We are just good friends."

They are such good friends that, in their own good time, they have a baby. This is a rather difficult spot. "I do know Miss Marston," admits Mr. LeRoy, "and I have a great admiration for her work."

And Miss Marston, holding the baby up to the camera so as to get a long-shot of the baby and a close-up of herself says: "I am terribly fond of Norman, but there is nothing in this talk of our engagement. We are just good friends."

And the first that we really hear of the marriage is when they are divorced. Perhaps this is why Hollywood divorces get so much publicity. It's the first time the couple has broken down and admitted being married.

Rule of Thumb

A LOT of us who were brought up on rhymes to aid us in memorizing academic rules and guides to living, find, as the years go by, that we are stuck with a lot of jingles with the key word missing. This can cause a lot of trouble.

I remember perfectly that "thirty days hath September, April, June and ———," but whether it is "November" or "December" is a mystery to me, and, although I have never been in a position where an extra day in a month, or an extra month in the year, made much difference one way or the other, I don't like to be in the dark like that.

I am letter perfect, except for one detail, on the old mariner's maxim: "——— skies at night, sailors' delight; ——— skies in the morning, sailors take warning." All that I *don't* remember is what color sky it is—blue, red or gray. Fortunately, I gave up my early idea of going to sea, otherwise all my clients might have ended up on the rocks and reeking of seaweed, especially as my only other nautical rule is "Mackerel skies and mares' tails make good sailors ——— ——— their sails." The nub of this advise is whether to "pull down" or "put up" their sails. That one point eludes me.

* * * * *

In spelling, I need every aid to memory that man can devise and even then I can whip up a few novelties by myself. I am more the inspirational type of speller. I work on hunches rather than mere facts, and the result is sometimes open to criticism by purists.

So it really is a matter for serious pause on my part when I remember "*i* before *e*, except after —" and am then confronted with *c*, *d*, *e*, *g*, *p*, *t* and *v* as possible rhymes. Also, I am not even sure whether it is "*i* before *e*" or "*i* after *e*." This practically vitiates the rule as a guide to spelling, whatever virtues it may have as a jingle.

In the study of foreign languages, I am equipped with several rhythmic grammatical rules which mean nothing, because I have forgotten the pay-off. In German, I can swing along on *aus, ausser, bei, mit, nach, seit, von* and *zu,* and I know that these words all are followed by the same case. But is it dative or accusative? That's what I can't remember!

In Latin (which, fortunately, I am not called upon to use in my work-a-day routine) I can recite *ad, ante, con, in, post, prae, pro, sub* and *super,* but, if you ask me whether it is the accusative, ablative, gerundive or putative case that follows them, I blush prettily and say, "See my lawyer!" You can't expect a man to remember *every*thing!

* * * * *

In the matter of drinking (which, thank Heaven, I do not have to worry about, now that we have Repeal!) there are several rhymes which can cause quite a bit of trouble.

Beer before wine,
Everything fine!

is all right as a slogan, unless you happen to think that it might be: "Beer *after* wine."

There is a world of difference there, my hearties! Ask any stomach specialist!

The trouble with rhymed rules is that the important words don't rhyme. The whole thing has got to be done over again, I'm afraid.

Old Suits for New

THE time is drawing near for my semi-annual humiliation before the clothing trade. When I go in to buy a new suit I must, according to an ancient blue-law which still survives, be wearing something. And, in my case, it is always an old blue suit.

Now, tailors hate old blue suits. They practically spit on them. Even if the suit came originally from them, they don't like it. If it has another tailor's name in it, it is all they can do to bring themselves to speak to you. And all my old suits are not only blue, but all came from different places.

I never got around to that well-ordered system of living where one always buys suits in the same place. I buy a new suit on the corner of the street where my old one begins to fall apart.

Sometimes, if I can stand still long enough without screaming, I have it made to order. Otherwise, I just go in somewhere and say: "A blue suit, please. Just send it!" and rush out. This gives one a bad name among the better class of tailors.

On whatever day I finally bring myself to enter a tailor's shop to be fitted for a new suit, I always seem to have on a model that I bought once in Augusta, Me., while on a fishing trip. It says "Pine Tree State Outfitters" inside the pocket. I keep thinking that I have thrown that suit away, but it always turns out to be on me when I go into a clothing store or a tailor's for a new rig. And the tailor thinks less than I do of it.

I begin taking the coat off before I am in the shop, and hide it under my arm so that he won't see the label.

Sooner or later, he spots it

But sooner or later, he spots it and the jig is up. From then on I have a hard time convincing him that I am not in the market for dungarees.

I once set fire to my dinner-clothes when I was in Rome and had to have a new set made. The man who recommended me to his tailor said: "Be sure to tell him that I sent you. He is very fussy about whom he makes clothes for. He refused to make a suit for a well-known movie actor once because he didn't like the Hollywood cut of the suit he was wearing."

This did nothing to reassure me, but I had to have the suit and knew of no other place to go.

On visiting the tailoring establishment of the great man, I found that he didn't speak English and thought that I was a button salesman. An accomplished assistant, however, translated to him that Mr. Doaks had sent me, and he asked me to step into his private office. As I crossed the threshold I realized that I had on a ready-made suit which I had bought in Hollywood! The skylight was too high up for me to jump through, and the door was already closed behind me.

The maestro looked me up and down, and made some crack to his assistant in Italian. The assistant laughed a nasty laugh, and told me to take off my coat. Although it is customary to take off one's coat while being measured for a suit, I had somehow hoped that I could avoid it this time. I thought some of saying that all I wanted was the trousers, but he wouldn't have liked that, I was sure.

So I took my coat off and doubled it up quickly, and tried to shove it casually under a bolt of cloth on the table. Then followed a series of quick maneuvers on the part of the assistant and me, he trying to get a look at the label, I fighting my heart out to prevent him.

While I was being measured he took a peek, and

then came out with another crack in Italian which sent his master into stitches and threw me into a state of furious blushing. I kept hearing the name of the friend who had sent me introduced into the badinage, and gathered that they thought he had been playing some sort of joke on them. So, as a joke, they went through with the horrid business, and I got my dinner clothes.

I still have that suit, and I think that when I go to get my new blue suit this Spring I will wear it to the tailor's. At any rate, he can't sneer at the label.

Taking Up the Cudgels

SOMEBODY named Sir Shah Sulaiman, of Allahabad, India, has seen fit to challenge Professor Albert Einstein's Theory of Relativity. In the absence of Professor Einstein, I am taking the liberty of replying in his behalf.

Einstein's value of the deflection of light from a star as it comes past the sun is 1.75. Sir Shah Sulaiman's prediction of value is between 2.32 and 2.45.

My answer to Sir S. S.: You're crazy.

Einstein's value of the amount of shifting toward red of the spectrum of the light from the limb of the sun is: .0084. Sir S. S. predicts that it will be found to be .00676.

My answer: Poppycock.

Sir S. S.'s third prediction concerns the elements of orbits of planets. He says that the value for the advance of the perihelion of planet Mercury is less than estimated by Newcomb.

My answer: Where is Allahabad, India, anyway? And who asked *you* to butt in on this? We were getting along very nicely with Prof. Einstein, who has proven himself to be an extremely pleasant gentleman and an all-around good egg. He also plays the violin. What can *you* play?

* * * * *

That is the trouble with discovering something worth while. Sooner or later some fly-by-night chief justice of India (that's what Sir Shah is, a chief justice) comes along and says that you are all wrong, and that he has discovered something better that will also cure head colds. Its enough to make a man like Einstein throw the whole thing up and just sail boats all the rest of his life.

Of course, it's none of my business, but, being in more or less the same line of work as Einstein (writing), I feel that we all ought to stand together.

Prof. Einstein probably will have something more to add to his own defense than what I have outlined here, but this will serve as an opening gun in the rebuttal.

I also hereby offer to meet Sir Shah in public debate.

The Party Spirit

O F ALL things to come into my hands at this time, closeted in a compartment on a train in the middle of a desert, is an article entitled: THE PARTY SPIRIT. The subhead to this article is as follows:

Something New, Something Quick,
But Also Tasty and Very "Trick."

The word "trick" is in quotation marks.

All right. Here is what is considered "something new, something quick, but also tasty and very 'trick' ":

Emerald Sundae: Dip ready-made marshmallow whip over chocolate ice cream. Sprinkle with green rubyettes, first carefully cut into tiny bits.

Let us leave out the matter of "rubyettes." I don't know what they are, but I can guess. And let us overlook the fact that the only Party Spirit I could display in this compartment would be to open and shut the closet door with one hand and turn on the hot water with the other, singing, "Hail, Hail, the Gang's All Here," the while.

The fact still remains that the trouble with a lot of parties today is that people read too many articles on the Party Spirit and cut too many rubyettes up into tiny bits.

There used to be a time, so I am told, when people

who gave a party didn't know what the "Party Spirit" was. They just asked in a lot of folks and dragged out a steer or two, whipped up a little sauce made of mustard

I would always be tiptoeing around with pencils

and just let people dip in. At least, we are given to understand that's what went on. I never gave such a party myself.

In fact, I don't give many parties, a fact which is commented on by people to whom I am indebted. "Why doesn't he ever give a party himself?" is the way they phrase it.

Well, I will tell you. I am afraid to. I am afraid that it would be a flop. I'm afraid that people wouldn't like what I gave them to eat. And, above all, that "Party Spirit" worries me.

Suppose I got a houseful of people and there turned out to be no "Party Spirit," as well as no food that anyone wanted to eat! Suppose there even turned out to be no people!

I would be one of those worrying hosts who get people out under the stairs and ask: "How do you think it's going?" I would always be tiptoeing around with pencils asking people to write down the name of the first country which comes into their minds and then forgetting how the rest of the game goes. I might even have hysterics and have to be taken upstairs.

It's this constant reading about how to get the "Party Spirit" and how to cut up rubyettes into tiny bits that gets me down. I just haven't got the knack.

Literary Forum

HOW does one get into a good conversation, or even get to listen to good conversation? By "conversation" I mean "argument," a good, knock-down-and-drag-out argument.

Most of the arguments to which I am a party fall somewhat short of being impressive, owing to the fact that neither I nor my opponent knows what we are talking about. I find myself raising my voice and shaking my finger, while he sneers and makes a sweeping gesture of disgust; but, to the onlooker, the thing must lack a certain authenticity.

And is there anything more fatuous than a loud argument in which you are not taking part? You sit and smile in a superior fashion at the two debaters, and even wink at other non-participants to show that at least *you* are keeping your head in this imbroglio. The fact that obviously neither one of them is making sense will give you a tip-off as to how you yourself sound to others when you enter the lists.

Just for the fun of it, I should like to have heard George Moore, Freeman and De la Mare arguing on the test of pure poetry. On second thought, I take that back. I bet that it wouldn't be any fun at all. It might have been more fun had they used the debating technique in vogue in the little circle of great minds that I move in. Their knowledge and our technique. Sub-

218

ject: Test of Pure Poetry. Rules: Marquis of Queensberry.

Moore: A true poem is something which a poet creates outside his own personality.

De la Mare: That's what *you* think!

Moore: That's what I say! Subjective poetry is not true poetry, and whaddya think of *that*?

De la Mare: Nerts!

Moore: I suppose you think that settles it!

De la Mare: It settles it as far as I am concerned. There never was anything to be settled.

. . . (*Pause while each one thinks up a crack*) . . .

De la Mare: What about Shelley?

Moore: Well, what about Shelley?

De la Mare: I suppose you think that Shelley wasn't a subjective poet.

Freeman: Yeah—what about Shelley?

Moore: Aw, you're both crazy!

Freeman: Subjective—objective—what do you mean? Do you know the difference?

Moore: Do *I* know the difference? Do *you* know the difference, you mean.

Freeman: Don't worry—*I* know the difference.

Moore: Well, then, talk as if you did. I suppose you think that Milton was an objective poet!

De la Mare: In just about everything he ever wrote, that's all!

Freeman: Yeah, Walter's right!

Moore: You keep out of this!

Tony: What'll you gentlemen have to drink? This is on the house!

(*All laugh, and order a pitcher of Black Velvet.*)

219

Sluggards, Ahoy!

AT A recent so-called "hobby exhibit" in New York a young man entered as his hobby a colony of ants. I remember thinking at the time: "Well, sir——"

Presumably the young man, who was specializing in zoology, took up ants as a hobby because he subscribed to the age-old theory that Man has a great deal to learn from the ants. As a matter of fact the only thing that I ever learned from an ant was not to try to carry too big a crumb on my back or I would walk sideways.

And now along comes as smart an ant-watcher as Professor Julian Huxley, who says that we humans can not only hold our own with ants, but possibly might be able to slip over a couple of tricks on them once in a while.

* * * * *

"One of the important differences between a human being and a termite is the matter of size," says Professor Huxley, cracking down with a dictum. "*Important* difference," Professor? It's colossal! It's the difference between my sleeping in my bed or an ant's sleeping there, that's all.

"If we had ants as big as fox terriers and wasps as big as eagles," continues Dr. Huxley—but there I left him. I don't want to know what the end of that sentence was. And I don't want anyone ever to begin a sentence that way again, either—at least, not within my hearing.

The comforting thing about Prof. Huxley's lecture was the statement that we really don't have to learn anything from the ant. We can go our way and the ant can go his. Contrary to our teachings, we do not have to be bending over all the time studying how the ants do it.

*   *   *   *   *

Human beings and ants have a great many things in common, however. They are the only organisms which have rubbish heaps, slaves and domestic animals, and which make war with military precision. Which brings me to a remark of Mrs. Patrick Campbell's, as what doesn't?

Mrs. Campbell was sitting at dinner next to an ant-watcher, who was telling, at considerable length, about the remarkable organization of ant communities.

"They have teams and working units, with subdivisions of labor," he said. "An ant community even has an army."

"No navy, I suppose?" asked Mrs. Campbell.

Which just about fixes the ants.

Who Killed Alfred Robin?

O NE of the myriad traits which distinguishes me from the nation's Great Men is my inability to finish a detective story. I can get right up to the last ten pages, but there galloping indifference sets in and I go out to the ice-box.

I can go for the first part of a detective story, where they are tripping over corpses and guilty-looking characters, and I perspire like a good one during the middle portions when screams and pistol shots are ringing out like chimes and Scotland Yard is biting its nails. But when it comes time for everything to be cleared up, and the detective explains just why he came to the conclusion that Scarboro did it I suddenly realize that I don't even know what the characters' names are, and that, furthermore, I don't particularly care.

I think that it is this question of characters' names that throws me off. As the story progresses, and more and more strange people are introduced, I get a little slovenly about filing them in my memory. I can't retain more than about five names, and, beyond that, I just trust to luck that I shall remember who they are when they come up again. Consequently, when I come to six solid pages at the end of the book which contain nothing but McCarthys, Wallaces, Martissis and Waldheims I naturally am at a disadvantage.

Following, if you are at all interested, is what the

last ten pages of most detective stories seem like, to me:

"Well, tell me, Inspector, what made you first suspect that it was Reedy and not Peroni who was at Balinto's place that night?"

"It was fairly simple, once we had established the fact that Gilgo could not possibly have been in Chicago with the Matessi gang. O'Rourke and Bleeker we knew were hard up—Greggory told us that—and Maude Marston had been working Dominic to get him to double-cross Vancy. *Now*—on the night when Freebish was seen coming out of Honfnagle's apartment——"

"But it was McCorck who was seen, wasn't it? That was what Teemy reported."

"Teemy reported it because he was afraid that if Clark knew that Noglatz had been playing around with Elsie he would tip off the Gorelli bunch and Szcynocyz would squeal."

"Then you didn't positively know that Glack was in the tannery that night?"

"I suspected it, but it wasn't until we found the pawn ticket in Vanderhook's overcoat that we knew that Duchy was in with Levine and Sabisty. Alice Gratz knew, but she couldn't talk because she was afraid of McNamara."

"But what about the insurance policy?"

"The insurance policy, if you will remember, was made out to Osterville, and the dog belonged to Pasterton. It was the dog that really gave the whole thing away."

"Well, I'll be darned!"

"No, I wouldn't say that exactly. But you'll buy me a drink."

I know that it is a peculiar lack of concentration on my part that makes me so susceptible to brain-fag at the end of detective stories, for millions of people the world over seem able to remember characters' names and to react when they appear in the printed page.

But, so long as I get a certain amount of simple-minded enjoyment out of the first chapters, when the murder is committed, and can follow along with my forefinger over the more exciting developments of the plot, what difference does it make who really committed the crime? If I don't care, who does? It's my book, and I may do with it as I like.

Maxims from the Chinese

THREE crows are there, if only there were three crows. . . . Oh, well, anyway——!

* * * * *

The wise man moves fast, yet a great many times it is hard to catch him. This is because he has no soul. This is because he lives up there with all those radicals.

* * * * *

It is rather to be chosen than great riches, unless I have omitted something from the quotation.

* * * * *

One day Lee Fee was walking along the countryside, with his hands on his elbows. He was thinking, thinking, thinking. So far he has failed to interest us as a character.

"I am wondering," said Lee Fee aloud, in case anyone was asking him. "I am wondering what comes after 'W.'" And, as he wondered, Lee Fee walked, and, as he walked, he wondered, and pretty soon he didn't know *what* he was doing

Soon he came to Lee Fee, walking in the opposite direction. This put a stop to his monkey-business He was good and scared. But he said: "Well, easy come, easy go!" and tried to brush by himself. But that is no easier than it seems.

"We are getting nowhere," said the east-bound Lee

Fee to the west-bound Lee Fee. "Let's see if we can't come to some compromise. We are both sensible men, and there is a saying of Confucius that the sensible man goes but a short distance with himself before taking his own temperature. It is also said that eggs do not roll sideways. There is also an old saying——"

But when Lee Fee looked up, Lee Fee was gone. He just couldn't take it. Too much wisdom gets on the wise man's nerves.

* * * * *

It is often difficult to tell whether a maxim means something, or something means maxim.

* * * * *

Three women were keeping house. It was too rainy. The First Old Woman said: "What wouldn't I give for three wishes at this very minute!"

"Well, what *wouldn't* you give?" asked the Second Old Woman.

"I wouldn't give my new silk coat, and I wouldn't give the roast pigeon in my oven, and I wouldn't give *that*," replied the First Old Woman, snapping her fingers.

"And why wouldn't you give any of these things for three wishes?" asked the Third Old Lady, who had heard nothing of what was going on.

"Because, even if I had three wishes," replied the First Old Woman, dying, "what chance would there be of their being granted?"

A wish without the giver is bare.

* * * * *

The wise man thinks once before he speaks twice.

Forgotten Money

IT IS not generally known that many banks throughout the country are holding large sums of money, unclaimed by their rightful owners. If it were, the money wouldn't be unclaimed.

Ever since I heard about this strange state of affairs I have been cudgeling my brains to remember some bank account of mine which I might have forgotten. It would explain a lot of missing money that I haven't got now. I *know* I didn't spend it.

There were several bank accounts of mine which the *bank* forgot but none that I can recall, off-hand, where *I* was the dreamy party. I have sometimes forgotten that I *didn't* have a bank account, and have drawn checks on which not even the date was valid, but try as I will, I cannot think of any bank to which I would go and say: "Oh, by the way, whatever became of that old balance I had here some years ago?"

This, however, doesn't mean that the thing isn't possible. I am notoriously scatter-brained about money affairs. Just because I can't remember what I have done with my money is no reason why a bank should sit tight and say nothing about any sum of mine that may be eating its head off in their vaults. I can't think of everything.

The decent thing for any bank to do, if it finds itself with some old account of mine that I have overlooked, is to get in touch with me. I am at home practically

I have sometimes forgotten that I didn't have a bank account

all day every day and the telephone is right by my bed. It would be my pleasure to put on some clothes and go down to the bank myself to see about it if they would only let me know. I might not even wait to put on some clothes.

I have never used pass-books in my banking, as the cashier has usually said: "Never mind actually depositing this, Mr. Benchley. I'll just keep it in my pocket until you need it." Later on I began carrying it in my *own* pocket until I needed it. As a result, I have no actual written evidence that I have money in any bank at all.

But the more I read the article on forgotten bank accounts the more I am convinced that it is the answer to my missing money. Somewhere, in each of the cities I have lived in, someone has a lot of money which belonged to me. If the banks haven't got it, who has?

Come on, now, banks—'fess up!

How to Eat

NOT only does it look as if we were in for an era of expert wine-tasting-and-spilling, with connoisseurs hanging over our shoulders to make sure that our Chambertin 1921 is just exactly the temperature of somebody's body, but, along with it, we are being made food-conscious.

The gourmets and food experts are now in the saddle, and a man can't pick up his paper or magazine without reading the bad news that, all his life, he has been eating his cup-custard like a barbarian, and that the old *maître d'hotel* at Foyot's used to say that anyone who would eat cup-custard without a dash of *kirsch* over it, and a few chives, slightly warmed, needled into the top crust, would sell his grandmother to a river-boat captain.

With all the people there are who claim to know all about special eating tricks it is very funny that one strikes so few dishes which are really knockouts. All my life I have been going from place to place to get legendary dishes that are supposed to make me swoon the minute they are passed under my nose, and all my life I have been pretending to be bowled over by them. As a matter of fact I have been able to take practically all of them in my stride.

"Just go to this little place in the Rue Felix Potin," I am constantly being told, "and tell Jean that Mr.

Gerbish sent you, and that he is to fix you up one of those special fish and kidney tarts. He'll understand." So I go and tell Jean, and he understands, and the fish and kidney tart is brought in, under motorcycle escort with all sirens blowing and everybody else in the restaurant backed into the corners.

Well, it's all right. That's usually the best that can be said for it. But it seldom is anything to make you fall flat on your face about. Even if, as Mr. Gerbish told you, you hold one mouthful of it for half a minute, and drip four dashes of Angostura bitters and a quarter of a teaspoonful of melted butter into one corner of your mouth, and a sip of 1844 Madeira into the other corner of your mouth at the same time—it is still just fish and kidneys, and no better than any good fish and kidneys ought to be. Sometimes it isn't even as good.

I once went to dinner with an old gentleman who was famous throughout New England for his steak sauces. He wouldn't let the restaurant do anything but bring the steak to the table, along with eighteen or twenty different bottles, including the extract of something taken out of an East Indian idol. Then he would push back his hair and stand up and pour things on the steak, at intervals of ten seconds by the watch, dabbing on little pinches of savory and smears of unguents, until you would have thought he was making up the steak for a Chinese bandit role in a Pearl Buck picture.

When he had finished making the sauce he was too depleted to eat any of it himself and had to go and lie down in the trophy room. The net effect of his labors was that of a moderately good steak covered with lots of Worcestershire.

I have a little recipe for boiled eggs which I would like to pass on to you, for I know that any readers of this page are sticklers for the art of good cooking and the even greater art of eating it:

Take the eggs, which have been boiled exactly three and a quarter minutes (they boil an extra quarter of a minute in their shells while being brought in hot water from the kitchen, making a precise total of three and a half minutes before they are opened). Crack them with a spoon which has been warmed to the temperature of your thumb, being careful not to let little bits of egg-encrusted shell slip down the side of the cup, as this slows up the mixing, besides making rather more of a mess than you had planned. Then take a dab of butter, the size of a dab of butter, and place it perpendicularly on the upper surface of the eggs, followed by a dash of salt and a dash of pepper, performed with a left-to-right gesture.

Then plough the top surface of the egg under, until a whole new surface appears, and repeat the process of butter, salt and pepper, turning each prepared surface under and exposing a fresh one, until the whole egg content has been thoroughly mixed. Then, as a final fillip, give four sharp turns with the spoon, and wash your fingers.

And if you don't say that they are the best boiled eggs you ever ate—then maybe they aren't.

Phobias

THE discovery of phobias by the psychiatrists has done much to clear the atmosphere. Whereas in the old days a person would say: "Let's get the heck out of here!" today he says: "Let's get the heck out of here! I've got claustrophobia!"

Most everybody knows the name of the phobia that he has personally, and it is a great comfort to him. If he is afraid of high places, he just says: "Oh, it's just my old acrophobia," and jumps.

If he is afraid of being alone he knows that he has monophobia and has the satisfaction of knowing that he is a pathological case. If he keeps worrying, in the middle of a meal, about the possibility of being buried alive, he can flatter himself that he has taphephobia, and that it is no worse than a bad cold.

* * * * *

But there are some honeys among the phobias that don't get much publicity. There is, for example, phobophobia, which is the fear of having a phobia, even though you may not have one at the moment. This takes the form of the patient sitting in terror and saying to himself: "Supposing I should be afraid of food, I would starve to death!" Not a very pretty picture, you will admit.

Then there is kemophobia, or the fear of sitting too

close to the edge of a chair and falling off. People with kemophobia are constantly hitching themselves back in their chairs until they tip themselves over backward. This gives the same general effect as falling off the chair frontward, so they find themselves in a *cul-de-sac*.

Then there is goctophobia, or the fear of raising the hand too far and striking oneself in the face, with the possibility of putting an eye out. These patients keep their hands in their pockets all the time and have to be fed by paid attendants. A nasty complication arises when they also have nictophobia, or fear of paid attendants.

* * * * *

Some of the other little known phobias are octophobia, or fear of the figure 8; genophobia, or the fear of being burned on door-handles; kneebophobia, or the fear that one knee is going to bend backwards instead of forwards some day, and optophobia, or the dread of opening the eyes for fear of what they will see.

Tell us your phobias and we will tell you what you are afraid of.

Fiction Stranger than Truth

IS TRUTH stranger than Fiction? This is a question which has half the world at loggerheads and the other half at sixes and sevens.

Of course, in order to settle it, one must know just how strange Fiction is. Then, working backward from that, we can see how strange Truth is, and come to some orderly decision satisfactory to both sides. The thing to avoid is hard feeling.

Here are a few happenings in real life which certainly are strange. If you can match them with happenings in fiction, I shall be dumbfounded.

Take, for example, the case of the man in Bermuda who was walking along the street one day recently (1756) when he stepped into a pit which had been dug by some pirates to hide a keg of gold later in the day. On crawling out, in no very good humor you may be sure, he fell forward into another pit which had been dug by some other pirates for the very same purpose. (The street was known as "Pirate Pit Street" and was a hot-bed for buried treasures.) On pulling himself out of the second pit, in no better humor than before, he muttered to himself: "This sort of thing has got to stop." As he said this, he looked down into the first pit he had fallen into, and there he saw his own self, climbing out face to face with him! So he dropped back into the second pit and stayed there. Explanation: There were two pits.

A Philadelphia man who kept cows was one day doing his milking, and, being slightly hung over, was resting his head against the cow's side as he milked. Suddenly his ear which was pressed against the cow detected the sound of conversation being carried on in low tones. He stopped milking but kept his ear pressed tight, and was rewarded by hearing the talk change from sotto voce conversation to bitter argument, increasing in tone until he could distinguish every word. The subject of the quarrel seemed to be, as usual, a woman.

The man left his listening-post and led the cow to a butcher, and, when it had been killed and cut open, sure enough, there inside were two very small men arguing about a woman. The men were released on bail and the milkman went home, still puzzling.

Perhaps the strangest of all happenings in real life is the series of events which led a criminal to arrest himself and then escape from himself, after giving himself an ugly cut over the eye. James Gargey, of Ultimate, Pennsylvania, surprised himself in the act of tearing off steps from a house that he had just robbed.

His idea, according to a confidante of his, was to cover up his tracks and make it look like an inside job. In addition to being a clever thief, Gargey was Chief of Police of Ultimate, and, in his official capacity, was forced to arrest himself. (It was Gargey who gave W. S. Gilbert the idea for "The Mikado," for which he never got a nickel.)

Confronted by the necessity for both making an arrest and escaping, he went to a neighboring saloon (one of the saloons which did come back, in spite of the slogan "The Saloon Must Not Come Back") and treated himself to a series of concoctions invented by the bartender in an off moment when he was working on a new drink for the "Miss Pennsylvania" prize. Following these, our hero swung on himself, landing a neat left to the eye, and then, wrenching himself out of his grasp, ran pellmell down the street and hid in a Chinese laundry until the affair had blown over. A rookie policeman brought food to his superior while he was in hiding.

These little incidents in real life are, I think you will agree, as strange as anything in fiction, or, in case you think of them as fiction, as strange as anything in real life. The point is that they are pretty darned strange.

Love Among the Thinkers

Who remembers the old days when lovers in novels used to talk about Love to each other? That was before Sociology, Biology, Communism, and the Machine Age crept into the hearts of our young people and made Thinkers of them. It used to be so that a hero who could back a heroine into a corner and fix her with a bloodshot eye, muttering: "It's the Irish eyes of you, and the crimson lips of you, and the wanton way you have of tossing the hair of you, that's driving me mad!" was pretty sure to get the rest of the way without having to change cars. But in the modern novel the hero who is not a graduate of the Rand School of Social Science and who cannot talk Values and Gestalt Psychology, while the necking is going on, might just as well resign himself to picking threads off his sleeve for the rest of his life.

Sinclair Lewis' heroines do dabble in Sex now and then (they always manage, these intellectual women, to get around to a few of the old-fashioned fundamentals somewhere during the book, and in just about the same way that their poor dear grandmothers did, too), but they constantly keep one eye on the Ratio of Biological Compromise and, at any given moment during the affair, could whip out statistics showing that Woman, as an Economic Determinant, can be expressed in terms of Thermodynamic Energy.

H. G. Wells' heroes, although not above an occasional affair d'amour of fairly commonplace proportions, temper their dalliance with a note of serious-minded debate on the

Future of Man-As-We-Know-Him, with Special Reference to Hormones and Basal Metabolism, and, what is more, always seem able to find a young lady who will take the negative when Cupid's hour begins to drag.

It is an old story, this dialectic love-making, for Mr. Wells, for, as long ago as "Ann Veronica" he began mixing Woman's Rights with Baby Talk, but Mr. Lewis seems still fresh from what I am afraid his heroine would call the "Chem. lab." and the whole thing is to him a breathless experience in contemplative incontinence.

Let us suppose, for the purposes of this brief burlesque, that Ann Vickers meets Theodore Bulpington in the moonlight on the Day Nursery roof of the Stuyvesant Industrial Home, and that she feels the Urge to be a Woman, as even a social-worker must feel it when June brings the scent of far-off Devon wafting on the velvet waves of Night. How would they go about it?

But first we must go back to the days of their respective childhoods. (It is always necessary to begin with childhood days to show how many of the Spanish War songs and slang phrases the author remembers and to recall how funny people used to look on bicycles.)

[CHAPTER ONE]

THE strains of "On the Banks of the Wabash," as sung by three small children in high treble voices, had just died down, and the first automobile in Kasawaska Center, Wisconsin, had simultaneously turned the corner of Elm and Maple Streets to the jeering cries of "Get a horse!" from the enraged citizenry.

Ann Vickers, aged three, confronted her companion, Arthur Rogers, aged five, with a determined gaze.

"Your father is a capitalist," she said.

"Capitalism is the backbone of our financial structure," replied Arthur, bridling.

"You will live to regret that statement, Arthur," said Ann. "Let me see . . . I should say in about 1933 the institution of Capitalism would be facing the greatest crisis of its career."

"Dat's a dreat bid lie," piped up little Ernest Herlinger, whose father owned the Kasawaska Light and Power Company.

"Be quiet, Ernest," responded Ann, "what do you know about Economics?"

"My father says that your father is an Anarchist," put in Arthur, thumbing his nose at Ann.

"That's the trouble with you capitalists," replied Ann, putting an all-day-sucker in her mouth, "muddy thinking. An Anarchist believes in no laws at all. My father believes in laws, but humane laws. Anarchy would get us nowhere, and I'll bet you a hundred billion trillion dollars that, by the turn of the century, some Anarchist has assassinated President McKinley."

"Let's play house," suggested little Ernest.

And, with childish cries of glee, the three tots were off for an afternoon of romping.

[C H A P T E R   T w o]

It had been six years since Theodore Bulpington began thinking about Religious Persecution in the Middle Ages. Theodore was now seven, and he had come to the conclusion that Religious Persecution was Sumpin Awful. Nationalism was Sumpin Awful, too. So was Cancer. The world was full of Sumpin Awfuls. This

240

was what Theodore Bulpington decided as he lay on a cliff in Cornwall and watched the gulls swoop down on the local fishes. Gulls were Sumpin Awful, too.

But there was always Art. No matter how you felt about the Revocation of the Edict of Nantes, there was always Art, and a chap could go a long way with Aubrey Beardsley to back him up. A chap could go a long way anyway, provided he could hear Offenbach often enough and ate enough stewed fruit.

"Darwin was a mucker," said Billy Himmerdink.

"Rot!" said Theodore.

"Rot is all very well to say, but where has Evolution got us?"

"Out of the primordial ooze and slime for one thing. And very nearly into the Twentieth Century for another."

"Thanks for nothing," said Billy.

Billy was a Sumpin Awful, even though he was Theodore's cousin.

[CHAPTER THREE]

The roof of the Stuyvesant Industrial Home and Day Nursery was a silver sea in the moonlight. Theodore, standing very close behind Ann Vickers, placed one hand over hers as it rested on the parapet.

"It's funny—our meeting like this, I mean," he said.

"It's funny our not having met like this before," said Ann, without turning her head. "Woman is Man's logical mate."

"Aren't you being just a little old-fashioned?" asked Theodore.

Ann winced. "Old-fashioned" was a hard word.

"I have seen nothing in Krafft-Ebing to make me think differently," she said, laying her head ever so lightly back on his shoulder. Her hair had the odor of sweet-grass baskets.

"Since the Twelfth Century we have seen Woman come on apace," said Theodore, pressing his lips into its soft fragrance. "And yet hormones are hormones, just as ballots are ballots. You can't evade the issue by calling on Krafft-Ebing."

Ann turned so that her face was close to his.

"I have studied biology," she said, gently. "Biol. 3a and Biol. 4b in the University. It ruined my religion, but it gave me my soul."

Theodore placed his hands on either side of her face and tilted it up toward him.

"The Reformation began in 1517," he said, tenderly. "When Martin Luther drove that nail into the church door at Wittenberg, he drove it into the Heart of the World." Then he kissed her.

"You talk like a behaviorist," said Ann, as soon as she could move her lips. "Does it ever occur to you that when the machines have taken over our entire civilization, we—you and I—Man and Woman—will be left free to revert to the Pleistocene Age and just paddle about in the mud?"

"You darling!" he cried, kissing her again. "And does it ever occur to *you* that Science, Literature, Religion, Invention, and Discovery, all the shibboleths of our modern civilization, are but words—words—words? Are there no such things as Values?" His arms crushed her to him. He was strong and smelled of shaving-soap.

242

There was a long silence, while the sound of the traffic came faintly from below.

"I've been thinking, my darling," said Ann, finally. "Didn't the Reformation begin before 1517? I mean, *really* begin?"

"You silly goose," replied Theodore, holding her at arm's length. "Of course it did. It began when the first male dinosaurus dragged himself across the glacier-swept plain toward his lady-love. It began when Cro-Magnon Man picked up Cro-Magnon Woman and carried her away to his cave. It began when Abelard—"

"Careful!" warned Ann, smiling. "It came very near ending with Abelard, if you will remember."

And, to herself, Ann Vickers said, as she nestled closer to a tweed lapel: "Here you are, Miss Vickers, the result of centuries and centuries of progress, the fine flower of Womanhood, possessed of the right to vote (August 26, 1920), the right to call your soul your own (September 15, 1889), and the fine instincts developed by generations and generations of New England stock, and what are you doing with your hormones? You are a sport, that's what you are. Not a sport in the sense of a sporting person, but in the biological sense, as given in Webster, 'an animal or plant, or one of its parts, that exhibits sudden and spontaneous variations from the normal type.' That's what Webster thinks of you! That's what Susan B. Anthony thinks of you! That's what the God of the Israelites thinks of you! I am ashamed of you, Ann Vickers!"

While this soliloquy was going on, Theodore was pressing her closer and closer to his chest, which was not like the weak chest of Professor Dinwiddie, nor the pudgy chest of Robert Paster, nor the barrel chest of Dr. Wormser, nor any of the other chests which Ann Vickers, in her search for social justice and prison reform, had encountered as a part of her laboratory work. It was Theodore Bulpington's chest, and it was good.

At last he spoke. "I do not look for an actual revolution," he said. "Not a revolution of blood and arson, like that in France at the close of the eighteenth century. But, my darling," and he kissed her on the forehead, "the old price system must go."

She took his big, strong hand in her two little ones.

"Let's go inside," she said. "I have some good Scotch in my room . . . And it is getting chilly out here."

Voice Culture

HAVING a little trouble in getting my voice to register in an emergency, such as calling out the number of my floor in an elevator or asking questions of a policeman, I have been going through a little book called *Voice Culture*.

All that I really need is something that will help me get the first syllable out. After that, I can rattle on myself.

I am afraid that *Voice Culture* is not exactly my dish. I can't bring myself even to do the first exercise. See if you could:

"Stand erect, with the chest held moderately high. Place the thumbs just above the hips with the fingers forward over the waist to note the muscular action. Then inhale and exhale and make the sound of 'ah' and the sound of 'ah-oo-oh,' and then say 'wah-we-wi-wa' slowly ten or a dozen times."

"The student should stop at once if signs of dizziness appear," says the book, but it doesn't say how to explain yourself if your wife appears, or the man to fix the radio.

"I was just saying 'wah-we-wi-wa,'" would seem to be the simplest way out. Leave it up to them to figure out why.

There are sentences for practice by people in my class who have the "Weak Take-Off" or inability to

Or asking questions of a policeman

get started in the lower registers. You whisper them to yourself, until you can do them without husking up.

One of them is: "I can't tell just how it happened; I think the beam fell on me."

Another: "Ask the man next to you if he'll let me see his program."

Another: "Keep back; wait till I see if the coast is clear." (Not very nice people use that one, I am afraid.)

Here again comes the danger of someone's overhearing you asking what you said. You can't say: "I said 'Keep back; wait till I see if the coast is clear.'"

Oh, you *can*, of course, but on the whole I guess I'll struggle along with my voice the way it is.

I said: *"I guess I'll struggle along with my voice the way it is."*

Dogs and Public Service

THE meter-readers and collectors for the Consolidated Gas Company of New York City do not seem to have quite caught the knack of making friends with dogs. During the past year 198 of them were badly enough bitten to require medical attention. This sort of thing obviously couldn't go on, even from the dogs' point of view.

So the company has issued a book of instructions to its 20,000 employes. It is called "Dogs: How to Approach and Handle Them," and, according to *Time*, it contains the following rules:

1. Make a little noise, to let the dog know that you are coming.
2. Show no alarm at growls or barks. They are simply challenges.
3. Welcome the dog's acquaintance-making sniffs.
4. Make no sudden or unnatural movements.
5. Speak only in a confident, friendly voice.
6. Keep your hands off.
7. Impress the dog with the propriety of your visit.

These rules sound simple, but I should think that one or two of them would call for quite a bit of finesse. The last one, Rule No. 7, for example. How would you go about impressing a dog with the propriety of your visit?

My instinct would be to say to the dog, "in a confident, friendly voice" (Rule No. 5): "Come on over here on the steps a minute, old boy. I want to talk to you." Then, when you and he were comfortably seated, you could point out to him that every age and every country has had varying standards of what is proper and what isn't proper.

Skipping and singing, "I'm coming, I'm coming!"

"Propriety is a question of environment" you could tell him, "and it is only a very narrow-minded person who tries to impose his standards of propriety on others. And you don't want to be thought narrow-minded, do you, Were-wolf?"

And he would probably shake his head, possibly with his teeth still in the calf of your leg.

Then you could show him that, under our present

economic system (which is already undergoing radical changes), it is necessary for public service corporations to make collections and make repairs, and that, so long as we live under this system (a bad one, you agree), people like you must, of necessity, make periodic calls.

"You see that, don't you, old fellow?" you could ask, just before you faint. And, if he is any kind of dog at all he will be impressed with the propriety of your visit and let go.

Just what "little noise" could be made to let the dog know that you are coming (Rule No. 1) is another problem. You might begin skipping and singing, "I'm coming, I'm coming!" just as you get to the gate, or perhaps carry a zither with you and strum a few chords softly in the middle distance. Another good way would be to hide behind the gatepost and call out: "Guess who's here! Gassy-mansy!" and then appear slowly, wagging a finger coyly.

On second thought, perhaps that wouldn't be so good. It might come under the head of "unnatural movements," which are warned against in Rule No. 4. The business of welcoming the dog's "acquaintance-making sniffs" and speaking in "a confident, friendly voice" is all very well, and goes hand in hand with "showing no alarm at growls or barks." These are the tactics that I invariably adopt, but I sometimes wonder if they fool the dog. My cheery "How are ya, boy?" spoken much too loudly and with a great deal too much confidence, has often failed to impress even me, especially if the dog keeps on growling.

Dogs are no fools, and I have a feeling that they recognize the sham and have contempt for it. I think that it might be better just to shut your eyes and walk right by, without any "How are ya, boy?" at all. Then at least, you would be keeping your self-respect, if not the cuff to your trouser leg.

It is a difficult problem that the Gas Company faces, and an even more difficult one that its employees face. Why couldn't householders just be taught to make their own repairs, and have the company let the unpaid bills ride?

Stamp Out Schistosomiasis!

NOW that we have got everything else in the world fixed up and running nicely, it is high time that we pitched in and helped the Rockefeller Foundation stamp out schistosomiasis in Egypt. I feel like an awful piker for having let it go as long as this.

Schistosomiasis, or flatworm disease, has been going on since 2000 B.C. among the Egyptians, so we really aren't the only ones who have been letting it slide, you see. Four thousand years of schistosomiasis almost makes it look as if the Egyptians just didn't care, one way or the other. Perhaps the Rockefeller Foundation is being quixotic about the thing and butting in where it isn't wanted.

Dr. Barlow, who is leading the fight against flatworm disease (or "Benton's bleenie"), says that it is caused by snails, which would, on the surface, seem to be pretty fairly easy animals to keep away from. I mean, you wouldn't have to put up nets around your bed or keep slapping the way you have to do to ward off mosquitoes. If the snails in this district were carriers for any disease, I don't suppose that more than one or two people in the entire state would catch it. But the Egyptians seem to be pushovers for snails. It has been estimated that eighty-five per cent of the native population has schistosomiasis, which shows you how snails get around in Egypt.

It really isn't the snails who give the disease to all

those Egyptians, but a parasite worm which rides around on the snail, which makes it all the more complicated. (They *can't* be the same as our snails. They must be a lot more agile.) These flatworms, according to Dr. Barlow, who ought to know, lay their eggs, which are known as "miracidia," and they swim around until they find another snail (I may not be getting this right. It sounds a little repetitious to me). If they don't find a snail within twelve hours, they die. This ought to make their extermination easy, as all one should have to do would be to hide all the snails for twelve hours.

When the miracidia have entered the snail (I *have* got it wrong), they go through some sort of rigmarole and come out as microscopic creatures resembling a fork-tailed tadpole. (So far the Egyptians have not figured in the thing at all, as far as I can see.) These tadpoles swim around again until they find what is known as a "host." This is where the Egyptians come in. They are the most perfect hosts in the world.

But here again the time limit enters, and should make it even easier to keep the miracidia out of the Egyptians. If miracidia do not find a human host within twenty-four hours, they die. You would think that this alone would limit their menace to almost a minimum, provided their human hosts can run at all. Not even the strictest rules of hospitality make it incumbent on a host to stand still and let himself be eaten into by a miracidium.

The catch seems to be that the Egyptians are great hands to wade around in water, irrigation ditches, and such, and the worm is at liberty to come and go through any breaks in the skin around the ankles and feet.

Once they are in, cirrhosis of the liver is just around the corner. So much for the technical side of the fight against schistosomiasis.

I suppose that it has occurred to Dr. Barlow and his aides, if not to the Egyptians over a period of four thousand years, to wear rubber boots when they go wading. I wouldn't be so bold as to suggest this. I also suppose that there has been some attempt to do away with snails, but as the Egyptian snails seem to be a lot more capable than ours, it probably is not so easy to do. From all that I can gather about them, they would have to be shot at with rifles, on the wing.

So I really have no solution for the problem, in spite of my sincere desire to help the Rockefeller Foundation. But, as I said before, the Egyptians have got to do *some*thing for themselves. They can't go around being the same perfect hosts that they have been for centuries, and if they give a darn whether they have cirrhosis of the liver or not, they have got to take a little interest in the campaign and do their bit. With any coöperation at all on the part of the victims of schistosomiasis themselves, we ought to crash through with a victory before another four thousand years are up.

The big surprise about the whole thing to me is to find out that there *are* any Egyptians today.

Cocktail Hour

IT IS all very well for New York and other large cities to go cosmopolitan in their new-found freedom, and to sit at sidewalk cafes in the Springtime, sipping their *aperitifs* and *demiblondes*. That was to be expected with Repeal.

But I must, merely as a passer-by, ask ladies who run tea-rooms not to put signs reading: "Cocktail Hour" in the windows of their tea-shops at two o'clock in the afternoon. Two P. M. is *not* "cocktail hour," no matter how you look at it. The very suggestion is terrifying.

How would you like to be walking along a perfectly normal street, with the hot sun beating down on your new straw hat and a rather heavy corned-beef-hash-with-poached-egg from luncheon keeping step with you, and suddenly to look up and see, pasted on the window of a tea-shop, a sign reading "Cocktail Hour"? I am just putting the question to you as man to man.

If two P. M. is "cocktail hour" in a tea-shop, what do you suppose four-thirty P. M. is? No wonder those shops close early. By nine they would be a shambles.

Do you suppose that the habitues of these otherwise respectable places begin looking at their watches along about one-thirty, just as they are finishing lunch, and say to each other: "Almost cocktail time at the tea-room!" making a little ceremony of it, the way other people do at five-thirty? It can't be very formal, with so many going right back to work afterward. Just regular business clothes, probably. There'll be only the regular bunch there. You know, the cocktail crowd!

Unless a stop is put to this strange perversion of daytime hours, we shall soon be seeing little signs pasted in the window of our favorite breakfast counter reading: "Have you had your matutinal absinthe and wheat-cakes?" or "When you hear the signal, the time will be exactly ten forty-five A. M. Time for our Special Chartreuse and Brandy Whooperoo!"

If the tea-rooms conducted by ladies want to celebrate "cocktail hour" at two P. M. that is their own business, of course, but they ought not to be so doggy about it. They should quite frankly come out with signs saying: "Pick-Me-Up Hour! Whisky Sours and Bismarck Herring for Receding Heads!" or "Don't try to last the afternoon out in your condition. A Silver Fizz will at least keep your hat on." Don't be so delicate in the matter. Come right out for the Hangover Trade.

But please, *please,* don't ask us older boys to look at signs reading "Cocktail Hour" just as we are going back to work from lunch. We have got men's work in the world to do.

Our Busy Bodies

THERE is getting to be altogether too much activity that we don't know about inside the human body. Every day we are told of some new hellish change that is going on in our cells, chromosomes reproducing, "genes" ringing bells and blowing whistles, until, compared with what goes on in a living organism, closing night at the Chicago World's Fair was like a Monday afternoon in the Ceramics Room at the Art Museum.

It will soon be so that a man can't call his body his own without first consulting a lot of chromosomes and genes and other will-o'-the-wisps that he never even saw a picture of.

It wouldn't be so bad if we had any personal contact with these so-called units that are using our bodies for their pagan routs. A good microbe (and why aren't they called microbes any more?) who came out into the open under a microscope and shook hands with you was a pleasure to have around.

But these chromosomes and their little genes just tear about in our cells without giving us common courtesy. We don't even know that they are there until suddenly we start falling apart. The scientists tell us that they are what keep us from reproducing cows and chickens instead of boys and girls, but there must be *some* other reason. I don't need a chromosome to tell me what's what.

What makes me a little leery of all this gene and

257

chromosome talk is that, up until just recently, the gene has been frankly a theoretical entity in the minds of the scientists. They talked about "genes," but they didn't know that there were any such things. They admit this themselves. They could just as well have called them "gorls" or "narfs."

Then somebody got a fruit-fly drunk and, calling it a "drosophila melanogaster," took apart one of its chromosomes and claimed to have discovered 2,500 genes in it. In other words, they first talked about "genes" and then, to save their faces, discovered them.

The point is, however, that so many things are happening which we don't know about until somebody tells us. We accepted germ action, when it came along, and adapted ourselves to a certain amount of interior activity. As it turned out, they weren't so right even about the germs, for we have to keep changing our plans about them every year to keep in line with the new theories.

But this chromosome and gene racket makes one a little uneasy. Isn't there anything that a man can do to prevent this constant buzz-buzz-buzz inside him? Under these conditions, there isn't much incentive to individual initiative on the part of a human being. The only thing for him to do is just sit still.

Why don't we go back and begin all over again, and recognize only those organic changes that we can see, like mumps and pink-eye? There's enough to worry about right there. The rest are going to function anyway, and, as no man has ever reproduced a sheep or a chicken yet, let's just hold tight and hope for the best in the future.

My Personal Beaver

I HESITATE to mention the matter here, as I may be misjudged, and it really is something which concerns me, and me alone. Or so my lawyer says. But I simply have got to tell someone about my beaver. It is getting to be more than just a nuisance.

I call it a beaver, but that is really giving it the breaks. That is ascribing to it some definite shape and personality, and these things it definitely has not got. It hasn't got one single attribute that I like. All that I know about it is (and my lawyer tells me that I must be very careful not to say anything against it that I cannot prove in a court of law) that it keeps appearing in my house, or rather disappearing in my house. It is always darting around corners just as I look up, or behind beams just as I look down. It is this ability on its part to be either on the floor or on the ceiling which makes me think that it might possibly *not* be a beaver. No beaver that I ever heard of could dart around a beam on my ceiling.

It has, however, certain characteristics of a beaver; it is rather round and dark, and seems to have a broad, flat tail, although I would not swear to the tail. It might be a smaller animal of the same type following it. (Good night, I hope not! If there were two of them I *should* be discouraged.) But if it is a beaver, it is a rather old and lethargic one and one who ought easily be caught up with except that I have no desire whatsoever to catch up with it. "Live and let live" is all I ask.

I first noticed it one day when I was feeling rather rocky after a night of moving three buildings from one place to another. (They weren't placed right at all, and so we tore them down and built them where we thought

I saw this small animal disappearing behind the door

they ought to be. That sort of thing wears a man down.) I was looking at a strip of bacon with just about as dirty a look as anyone ever gave to a strip of bacon, when, glancing up to see if there might not be something in the bookcase that I would like to eat better, I saw this small animal disappearing behind the door. Now, I have not owned a small animal since my Scottie was arrested for inciting to riot in Union Square, and I have no friends who are small enough to dart behind a door 'way down there. So I naturally looked quickly away again, and thought nothing more of the matter, except to pace up and down the room all day in a cold sweat.

The next day I was weaving on a tapestry which I am trying to finish for the museum at Bayeux, when, on glancing up at the ceiling to try to think of which stitch came next, I saw the same small form whisk behind a beam, with just a suggestion of a tail protruding behind it. The tail was what made me say instantly to myself: "A beaver!" The ceiling was what made me say almost immediately afterward: "Beaver, my eye!"

This has gone on now for several weeks and I am frankly at a point where I would cry if anyone pointed a finger at me. I asked my lawyer what to do about it, and he said to say nothing to anybody, but to lie low. But you can't have a stray beaver around the house, on the floor *and* on the ceiling, without telling somebody. But not a word more will you get out of me.